I-L
Indians to Laotians

Titles in the series

The NEWEST Americans

I-L
Indians to Laotians

GREENWOOD PRESS
Westport, Connecticut · London

Library of Congress Cataloging-in-Publication Data

Creative Media Applications
  The newest Americans.
     p. cm.−(Middle school reference)
  Includes bibliographical references and index.
  ISBN 0-313-32553-7 (set: alk. paper)−0-313-32554-5 (v.1)−0-313-32555-3 (v.2)−
  0-313-32556-1 (v.3)−0-313-32557-X (v.4)−0-313-32563-4 (v.5)
     1. Immigrants−United States−Juvenile literature−Encyclopedias.
     2. United States−Emigration and immigration−Juvenile literature−Encyclopedias.
     3. Minorities−United States−Juvenile literature−Encyclopedias.
     [1. Immigrants−United States−Encyclopedias. 2. United States−Emigration and
     immigration−Encyclopedias. 3. Minorities−Encyclopedias.] I. Series.
  JV6455.N48 2003
  304.8'73'03−dc21   2002035214

British Library Cataloguing in Publication Data is available.

Library of Congress Catalog Card Number: 2002035214
ISBN: 0–313–32553–7 (set)
         0–313–32554–5 (vol. 1)
         0–313–32555–3 (vol. 2)
         0–313–32556–1 (vol. 3)
         0–313–32557–X (vol. 4)
         0–313–32563–4 (vol. 5)

First published in 2003

Greenwood Press, 88 Post Road West, Westport, CT 06881
An imprint of Greenwood Publishing Group, Inc.
www.greenwood.com

Printed in the United States of America

The paper used in this book complies with the Permanent Paper Standard issued by the
National Information Standards Organization (Z39.48–1984).

10 9 8 7 6 5 4 3 2 1

A Creative Media Applications, Inc. Production
WRITER: Sandy Pobst
DESIGN AND PRODUCTION: Fabia Wargin Design, Inc.
EDITOR: Susan Madoff
COPYEDITOR: Laurie Lieb
PROOFREADER: Betty Pessagno
ASSOCIATED PRESS PHOTO RESEARCHER: Yvette Reyes
CONSULTANTS: Robert Asher, University of Connecticut

Special thanks to Donna Loughran and Mary Ann Segalla
for their contributions to this volume.

PHOTO CREDITS:
Cover: © Najlah Feanny/CORBIS SABA
AP/Wide World Photographs *pages* 6, 19, 21, 22, 24, 29, 31, 33, 34, 37, 41, 42, 46, 49, 50, 53,
56, 59, 64, 67, 69, 73, 79, 80, 83, 84, 85, 87, 88, 91, 93, 98, 100, 103, 106, 109, 110, 113, 114,
117, 119, 122, 125, 129, 131, 133, 135
© Najlah Feanny/CORBIS SABA *page* 14
© Jose Fuste Raga/CORBIS /CORBIS *page* 38
© Robert van der Hilst/CORBIS *page* 96

Contents

America
is another name
for opportunity.

−Ralph Waldo Emerson

A Word about
The Newest Americans

This series takes a look at the people who have been coming to America from 1965 to the present. It provides historical, social, political, and cultural information on the most recent immigrant groups that are changing the face of America.

Charts and graphs show how immigration has been affected over the years, both by changes in the U.S. laws and by events in the sending country. Unless otherwise noted, the term *immigrant* in this book, including the charts and graphs, refers to new legal immigrants and to refugees and asylees who have changed their status to legal permanent residents.

From its very beginning, the United States stood for opportunity and freedom. It exists because immigrants, people who moved from their homes to make a new life in a new country, dreamed of better lives. They dreamed of having a voice in their government, of expressing their opinions and practicing their religion without fear of being imprisoned or tortured. Two hundred years later, these dreams still call to people around the world.

opposite:
Lance Corporal Daniel Njoroge Wanjoh is a citizen of Kenya serving in the U.S. Marine Corps. Because of an executive order signed by President George W. Bush on July 3, 2002, he and other foreign-born men and women serving in the U.S. armed forces are eligible for citizenship more quickly than they would be if they were not in the military.

E Pluribus Unum—

An Immigrant Nation

America declared its independence from British rule in 1776. At that time, nearly 80 percent of the people living in the colonies were white Europeans from England, Ireland, Scotland, Germany, the Netherlands, France, and Sweden. Just over 20 percent were slaves from Africa, the one group of American immigrants who did not come to this country willingly.

Over the next 200 years, more than 70 million people from around the world would *immigrate* to the United States. The majority came for *economic* reasons, eager to make the American dream a reality. Although this was one of the largest migrations of people in history, it began slowly. Wars in the United States and Europe kept immigration to a minimum until the 1820s. As things became more settled, however, a rapidly growing population that had few opportunities in Europe looked once more to America.

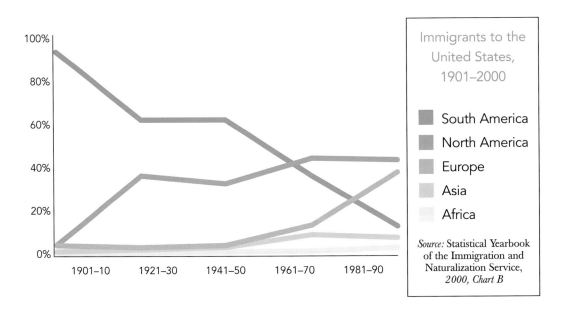

Immigrants to the United States, 1901–2000

- South America
- North America
- Europe
- Asia
- Africa

Source: Statistical Yearbook of the Immigration and Naturalization Service, *2000, Chart B*

Out of Many, One

—*Motto of the United States*

The 1800s

America offered freedom and political equality, but it also had practical attractions. Vast amounts of land unclaimed by white settlers, coupled with a growing number of jobs in the United States, exerted a strong pull on the imagination. Immigrants believed that they could improve their lives—and maybe even become wealthy—if they could only get to America.

There were many factors "pushing" immigrants to the United States as well. Population explosions, poor economic conditions, and widespread famine in Europe left many without work during the 1830s and 1840s.

The next big wave of immigrants reached American shores in the 1880s and 1890s. This time the newcomers included large numbers of southern and eastern Europeans. Immigrants from Italy, Austria-Hungary, Russia, and Poland began settling in America's cities and working in the factories.

Immigrant Chains

Immigrant chains form when members of one immigrant family settle in America, and then convince family members and friends to join them. The established immigrants help the new immigrants find homes and work in the same area. Immigrant chains have influenced settlement patterns all over the country, helping to create large communities of Cubans in Miami, Dominicans in New York, and Chinese in San Francisco, among others.

The 1900s

Immigration to the United States set a record in the first decade of the twentieth century. Nearly 9 million immigrants were recorded as entering the United States from 1901 to 1910.

For the first time, immigrants from southern and eastern Europe were in the majority. Many of these immigrants were Jewish and Catholic, in contrast to the predominantly Protestant groups that settled the United States. Immigration surged again from 1918 through 1921. Only when Congress enacted a quota system in 1921 and 1924 did immigration begin to decline. The *quota* system severely restricted the number of immigrants that would be allowed to enter the United States from each foreign country.

Immigration numbers remained low until the mid-1960s. But two events in particular caused America to rethink an immigration policy based on race and ethnicity. The first event was the *genocide* (systematic destruction) of European Jews during World War II. German leader Adolf Hitler's vision of a racially pure world was in direct opposition to the ideals the United States was based on. Yet the immigration policy was set up to admit primarily white Europeans. The second event was the American civil rights movement, which began in the mid-1950s and gained momentum in the 1960s. Many people felt that the United States, as a world leader, should adopt an immigration policy that would reflect its ideals of equality and freedom for everyone regardless of race or country of origin.

The Immigration and Nationality Act of 1965 introduced far-reaching changes in American immigration policy. The quota system was discarded in favor of worldwide limits. With family reunification as a priority, lawmakers allowed immediate family members of U.S. citizens to be admitted without limit.

Terrorist acts against the United States in 1993 and 2001 sparked changes to the immigration policy once again. The location of temporary (nonimmigrant) visitors, including students and businesspeople, is now being tracked more closely. The government has more freedom to investigate and detain suspected terrorists.

Immigration Today

In 2000, nearly 850,000 people became legal immigrants. Legal immigrants, also called legal permanent residents, receive paperwork, or documentation, that shows they are living in the United States legally. The documentation, commonly called a "green card," also allows a new permanent resident to work in the United States.

American immigration laws determine how many foreigners, or aliens, can enter the United States each year. Currently, the law allows between 421,000 and 675,000 immigrants to be admitted each year. Most of the yearly admissions are reserved for family-sponsored immigrants (up to 480,000 per year). People who have job skills that are in demand, such as scientists, software programmers, and computer analysts, are also among the first chosen. They qualify for the employment-based preferences (up to 140,000 per year).

Each year, 50,000 to 55,000 immigrants enter the United States through the Diversity Program. This program addresses the inequalities of past immigration policies. Residents of countries that have sent fewer than 50,000 immigrants to the United States in each of the past five years are eligible to participate. Visas, or permits, are issued to those applicants whose names are randomly selected, giving the program its common name—the diversity lottery.

Immigrant Admissions in 2000

a	Immediate relative of U.S. citizen	41%
b	Family preference	28%
c	Employment preference	13%
d	Refugee/asylee adjustment	8%
e	Diversity Program	6%
f	Other	4%

Source: Immigration and Naturalization Service

Immigration Legislation

Until the late 1800s, there were few federal restrictions on immigration. States had the ability to control or limit immigration. This changed in 1875 when the federal government gained control of immigration. Beginning in the 1920s, the laws also specified the number of immigrants that could come to the United States each year.

Here is a brief description of the laws that have changed American immigration patterns over the past 200 years:

1882   The *Chinese Exclusion Act* stopped nearly all new immigration from China. Chinese immigrants would not be admitted in large numbers again until the 1950s.

1907   The so-called *Gentlemen's Agreement* blocked most Japanese immigration. A presidential order kept Hawaiian Japanese from moving to the United States.

1917   The *1917 Immigration Act* required immigrants to pass a literacy test before entering the United States. It also created a zone covering most of Asia. No immigration from this zone was allowed.

1921   The *Quota Act* temporarily limited immigration after World War I. Immigration limits were based on national origin. Immigrants from the Western Hemisphere were not subject to limits.

1924   The *1924 Immigration Act* established the first permanent limits on immigration, continuing the national origins quota system. Before this law was enacted, the idea of illegal immigration did not exist.

1952   The *Immigration and Nationality Act of 1952* lifted some of the restrictions on Asian countries. Discrimination based on gender was eliminated. For the first time, preference was given to foreigners whose skills were in demand and to relatives of U.S. citizens and residents. Race-based limits were abolished when all races became eligible for naturalization.

1965   The groundbreaking *Immigration and Nationality Act of 1965* (also known as the Hart-Cellar Act) eliminated the quota system for worldwide limits.

1980   The *Refugee Act of 1980* established procedures for admitting and resettling *refugees*. It also made a distinction between refugees and asylees.

1986   The *Immigration Reform and Control Act (IRCA)* attempted to address the problem of illegal immigration. It provided an opportunity for immigrants who were living and working illegally in the United States before January 1, 1982, to adjust their status and eventually become legal residents and naturalized citizens.

1990   The *Immigration Act of 1990* made several major changes in U.S. policy. The total number of immigrants and refugees allowed to enter the United States each year increased dramatically. A Diversity Program allowed immigrants from countries that were underrepresented in America in the past an extra chance to receive a visa.

1996   The *Antiterrorism and Effective Death Penalty Act* outlined measures to identify and remove terrorists from the United States. It allowed the U.S. government to use evidence collected in secret to accuse immigrants of terrorist acts.

1996   The *Welfare Reform Act* was designed to keep most legal immigrants from getting food stamps and supplemental security income provided by the federal government.

1996   The *Illegal Immigration Reform and Immigrant Responsibility Act* focused on improving control of the U.S. borders.

2001   The *U.S.A. Patriot Act* expanded the government's ability to investigate, arrest, and deport legal residents for failing to comply with immigration regulations. Immigrants (including legal residents) who were suspected of terrorism could now be held indefinitely in detention centers.

Refugees and Asylees

Some people have to leave their countries because it isn't safe to live there anymore. Those who are afraid to return to their country because of persecution ask countries like the United States to take them in. People who are living outside the United States when they apply for protection are called refugees. They often have to wait years before their application is granted. The number of refugees permitted to resettle in the United States each year is determined by the president after discussions with Congress.

Like refugees, asylees are also seeking *asylum,* or safety from persecution. The difference is that asylees make their way to the United States before they ask for asylum. Most asylees come from countries that are located near the United States, such as Cuba, Nicaragua, and Guatemala.

Illegal Immigrants

In addition to the nearly 1 million legal immigrants who arrive in the United States each year, hundreds of thousands of people enter the country without permission. No one really knows how many illegal immigrants enter the United States each year. The Immigration and Naturalization Service (INS) estimates the number at close to 300,000 per year. These immigrants don't have the papers (visas) that show they have been admitted legally to the United States. They are often referred to as undocumented aliens or illegal immigrants.

In 1996, the INS estimated that 5 million undocumented immigrants were living in the United States. Today, experts suggest that the number is between 6 and 9 million. Over half are from Mexico. Because it is easier for people from nearby countries to enter the United States illegally, eight of the top ten countries sending illegal immigrants are in Central America, the Caribbean, and North America. The other two are the Philippines and Poland.

Becoming Naturalized Citizens

Amerian citizens enjoy many rights that permanent residents and visitors do not have. American citizens have the right to vote to select their leaders. They may hold government jobs and run for elected office. They can ask the government to allow family members to come to live in the United States. American citizens can also apply for a U.S. passport, making it easier to travel abroad.

Anyone who is born in the United States is automatically a citizen. Immigrants who want to become citizens must go through a process called naturalization. Before permanent residents can become naturalized citizens, they must live in the United States for a specified amount of time, usually three to five years. Once the residency requirement has been met, the resident must submit an application to the INS. A criminal check is completed during the application process.

The next step is an interview between the applicant and an INS officer. The ability to speak English is judged throughout the interview. Questions about the history and government of the United States test the immigrant's understanding of American civics. At the end of the interview, the officer either approves or denies the application for citizenship. An applicant who fails one of the tests may be given a second chance to pass the test.

Applicants who successfully complete the naturalization process attend a naturalization ceremony at which they swear an oath of allegiance to the United States. Each new citizen then receives a Certificate of Naturalization. Children under eighteen automatically become citizens when their parents take the oath of allegiance.

opposite:
More than 300 of the newest Americans wave flags following their citizenship swearing-in ceremonies on Ellis Island in New York harbor. Many immigrants first set foot in the United States on Ellis Island during the nineteenth and early twentieth centuries. It is now a favorite place to take the oath of citizenship because of its rich immigrant heritage.

American Attitudes toward Immigration

Throughout America's history, immigrants have been both welcomed and feared. Negative attitudes toward immigrants tend to increase when the economy is in a slump. Increased competition for jobs and fears for the future lead many Americans to close ranks.

Discrimination

From the start, immigrants faced *discrimination* in America regardless of their race. Irish-Catholic, Japanese, Chinese, and Filipino immigrants have all been targets of hostility through the years.

Immigrants today continue to struggle to fit in. They are judged by their ability to speak English, their skin color, their clothing. Immigrant children comment that their new English vocabulary includes words like "discrimination," "prejudice," and "stereotype."

Immigration Myths and Realities

The debate over immigration has been heated from time to time. Amazingly, the same arguments against immigration have been made for over 100 years. Below are some of the claims that are often made about immigrants. The facts are also given.

Myth	*Reality*
Immigrants take jobs away from Americans.	New immigrants usually accept low-paying jobs that Americans don't want or won't accept. Immigrants often revitalize urban areas. Many open new businesses, providing jobs for others.
There are too many immigrants today. They outnumber Americans.	The actual number of immigrants in recent years does exceed that of past years. Immigrants in the 1990s, however, made up less than 3 percent of the population, compared to 9.6 percent from 1901 to 1910.
Immigrants come to America because they want to receive financial assistance, called welfare, from the government.	New immigrants must prove that they won't be a burden before they are allowed to enter the United States. Historically, new immigrants are more likely to be employed, save more of their earnings, and are more likely to start new businesses than native-born Americans. Recently, however, the percentage of immigrants receiving welfare is nearing that of native-born Americans.
Immigrants keep to themselves and speak their own languages. They don't want to be Americans.	Immigrants know that English is the key to success in the United States. Classes teaching English as a second language fill up quickly. There is usually a waiting list. Studies show that children of immigrants actually prefer English.
There is too much diversity among immigrants today. *Ethnic* enclaves, or communities, mean that immigrants don't have to adapt to the U.S. *culture*.	Some social scientists argue that *ethnic* enclaves form when immigration is not diverse enough.

The Immigrant Experience

Destinations

All immigrants to the United States have to make life-altering decisions that will change the course of their future. Their decisions are usually based on three main factors: location of family members, if any; opportunities for work; and proximity, or closeness, to their home country. These three factors have influenced settlement patterns since immigrants first began arriving on America's shores.

Although immigrants can live anywhere in the United States, nearly two-thirds of them settle in just six states. California, New York, Florida, Texas, New Jersey, and Illinois count more immigrants among their population than all other states combined. California alone is the destination of one-fourth of the nation's immigrants.

Because finding work and living near others who share their experience is so important, nearly all new immigrants (93 percent) live in urban areas. The most popular U.S. destinations in 2000 were New York City, Los Angeles, Miami, Chicago, and Washington, D.C.

Refugees do not necessarily follow these same settlement patterns, at least when they first arrive. As part of their relocation package, they are resettled into communities across the United States. Individuals or families in that community *sponsor* the refugees, helping them get used to their new surroundings. When refugees adjust their status to immigrant, they often choose to move to a location with a larger immigrant community.

Immigrant Destinations

a	California	25.6%
b	New York	12.5%
c	Florida	11.6%
d	Texas	7.5%
e	New Jersey	4.7%
f	Illinois	4.3%
g	All other states	33.8%

Source: Immigration and Naturalization Service

Fitting In

Social scientists call the process of adapting to a new culture *assimilation*. Assimilation takes place over time and in different ways. There is economic assimilation, in which immigrants take advantage of workplace opportunities to increase their income. Social and cultural assimilation take place as immigrants form friendships with Americans at school and at work. English skills improve and cultural traditions from their home country may be adapted. Young people especially become immersed in the American culture and begin to adopt those values. Finally, there is political assimilation. This occurs when immigrants choose to complete the naturalization process so their voices can be heard in their government.

CHAPTER ONE

Indians

India,

a large country west of China, is a country of many contrasts. Its history of invasions by foreign *conquerors* and its location along major trade routes have created an interesting mix of people in India. Today, many groups still practice their ancient traditions and speak their own languages. India has fifteen official languages. The main language, Hindi (HIN-dee), is spoken by about one-third of the people. Although English is not an official language, it is commonly used in government and business.

Immigrants from India have been called by many names in the United States. The term "Indian" was used to refer to Native Americans until recently, so early immigrants from India were often called "East Indians." Early immigrants were also called "Hindus." (Hindustan was an early name for India.) The name "Hindu" was confusing, though, because it also refers to followers of the Hindu religion. In recent years, the term "Asian Indians" has been used. In this chapter, since we focus on India, the name "Indian" will be used.

Language

Over 200 languages are spoken in India. Twenty-four of these are spoken by at least a million people.

One out of Six

India is the most crowded country on Earth. About one-third the size of the United States, India is home to one out of every six people on the planet.

A Quick Look Back

I ndia is the site of one of the world's ancient *civilizations*. The earliest settlers, around 2500 B.C., were probably a group of people called the Dravidians. They are believed by some to be the native Indian race. The Aryan people arrived in India about a thousand years later. The Aryan people originated in southeastern Europe. Some of them moved into northern Europe. A group of them moved south into Asia. After thousands of years and many changes in their ethnic makeup and beliefs, they moved southeast into Persia, Afghanistan, and India. They introduced Hinduism and the caste system.

A Dalit, or untouchable, pulls a cart with heavy materials through the streets of New Delhi. Dalits are the lowest of India's five castes and are often relegated to menial or difficult jobs.

The Caste System

Imagine that the family you were born into would determine what you could eat and wear, where you could work, or whether you could enter a temple for worship. This is what the caste (kast) system meant in ancient India. According to Hindu law, people in one caste could not marry or socialize with people in another caste. Although the caste system is illegal in India today, many people still follow its principles, especially in the rural areas

From highest to lowest, the four castes introduced by the Aryans around 1500 B.C. were the Brahmans (priests, government officials), the Kshatriyas (warriors, rulers), the Vaisyas (merchants, farmers, traders), and the Sudras (artisans, laborers, servants). Later, a fifth caste was added—the Untouchables, known today as the Dalits or "broken people."

The Dalits are considered the lowest level of society. In the past, they could not own land and were assigned jobs no one else would do, such as cleaning toilets

and burying the dead. In India today, over 160 million people are Dalits. It has been hard for them to break out of the poverty of their circumstances. They are beginning to organize and build political power, but they still face extreme discrimination from people in their immediate regions. who consider themselves upper-caste.

Islamic conquerors arrived in India in the tenth century and converted many Indians, especially in the northwestern Punjab region. South India remained primarily Hindu, although a small number of people converted to Islam. For the next six centuries, warfare was a way of life as invaders fought to gain control of India.

In the early sixteenth century, Babur, a descendant of earlier Mongol conquerors, established the Mogul (MOH-gul) *Empire* in northern and central India. (It is also known as the Mughal Empire.) Under the leadership of Babur's grandson Akbar, the Mogul Empire became as famous for its music, art, architecture, and literature as for its military skill. Akbar and his *descendants* ruled India until the early eighteenth century. While the Mogul Empire officially ended in 1858, its last century was full of chaos as the once great regime splintered into smaller states and kingdoms.

British Rule

European countries began establishing trade routes to India in the seventeenth century. The British East India Company was the first to arrive, followed by Dutch and French traders. By the end of the eighteenth century, this company controlled most of southern Asia, including India. Most trading posts were along the southern coast. The British bought Indian spices, such as black pepper, cinnamon, and cardamom, and fine cotton cloth.

The Taj Mahal

The Taj Mahal, one of the eight wonders of the world, was built by the grandson of Akbar, first ruler of the Mogul Empire. When the emperor Shah Jahan's favorite wife died in 1631, he built her tomb of white marble and called it the Taj Mahal (*tazh* ma-HAL). Nearly four centuries later, it still gleams white in the sunlight. It changes color throughout the day, reflecting the pink of sunrise and the silver moonlight.

Shah Jahan hired the best architects and artisans in the region to build the Taj Mahal. A thousand elephants helped move the building materials from across India to the construction site in Agra. The tomb took twenty-two years to build and required 20,000 workers. The main dome rises 213 feet (64 meters) high, higher than a modern twenty-story building. A ramp two miles (3 kilometers) long enabled workers to get the stones up to the level of the dome. The Taj Mahal attracts millions of visitors each year.

The growing British influence directly affected the livelihood and income of the Indian people. The Indian cotton textile industry was virtually shut down during British rule; the British began sending raw cotton directly to England to support its own growing textile industry. People who had independently supported their families for generations were now dependent upon the British for work and goods.

A number of British citizens settled in India in the early nineteenth century. Unlike the earlier traders who had accepted and adapted Indian customs, the new arrivals looked down upon Indian religions and traditions. By 1835, English had become the language of government in India. The British began an educational system for Indian children to cement the British Crown's control in the region. The children were taught the English language, British customs, and loyalty to Queen Victoria. The brightest children were sent to England for higher education. Some wealthy Indians sent their sons to English universities. These few might aspire to lower-level secretarial and accounting jobs with the British government in India.

As the East India Company's control grew stronger and more widespread, Indians began to rebel. After the Sepoy (SEE-poi), or Soldier's, Revolt was crushed in 1858, the British Crown took over formal control of India. The Sepoy Revolt is also known as the first War of Independence.

The number of poor Indian families increased dramatically in the late 1800s. At the same time, British colonists were growing wealthier. Indians began calling for more representation in their government. They demanded that they be given the same rights and responsibilities as other British citizens. As the twentieth century began, the British began to allow more local self-government. They recognized the Indian National Congress, a newly formed political party. But these small freedoms allowed by the British government only made the Indian people want more.

Struggle for Independence

After World War I, the British enacted reforms that gave Indians more involvement in the government. But new laws against "revolutionary activities"–generally anything that threatened the British power structure–limited the Indians' freedom to protest.

Mohandas Gandhi (GAHN-dee), an Indian political leader, used his law degree to fight for Indian independence from Britain. He encouraged peaceful strikes against British policies in India, uniting Hindus, Muslims, and Sikhs in their desire for freedom.

Spotlight on
MOHANDAS GANDHI

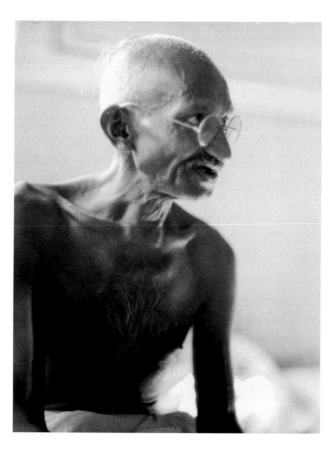

Mohandas Gandhi, leader of India's movement for liberty, is shown one hour after being released from the British government prison in Poona, India. Gandhi did not like being photographed and rarely looked directly at the camera.

Mohandas Gandhi, a leader of the Indian struggle for independence, became one of the most influential people in the world. People called him Mahatma (muh-HOT-muh), which means "great soul." Gandhi believed that it is wrong to hurt another person. He thought that the best way to make the British leave India was to refuse to obey unfair laws. He called this policy "passive resistance."

Gandhi's movement gained momentum in 1919 when British troops shot and killed hundreds of Hindus who were peacefully celebrating a religious festival. For the next few years, Indians followed Gandhi's lead by boycotting nearly everything British. They didn't attend British schools, buy

British goods, or travel on British transportation systems. In 1930, when the British put a tax on salt that made it too expensive for poor Indians, Gandhi decided to walk over 200 miles (over 322 kilometers) to the sea and make salt himself. Thousands joined him in his march to the sea. Seeing strength in numbers, the British released control of India in 1947.

Gandhi's example of nonviolence has influenced many people, including many world leaders. Dr. Martin Luther King Jr. successfully used Gandhi's methods during the American civil rights movement.

In 1947, Jawaharlal Nehru (NAY-roo) became India's first prime minister. Britain oversaw the difficult transition of power. Almost immediately, differences between Muslim and Hindu leaders led to the division of India into two separate nations. Muslims were afraid that their concerns would be overlooked in the new country since they were a religious minority. They lobbied Britain and the transitional government for a country of their own. The country of Pakistan was born out of this conflict and became home to most of the Indian Muslims. This religious conflict led to violence and bloodshed. One million Hindus and Muslims were murdered or killed in battle, and many *refugees* were forced to *emigrate* or face religious discrimination.

Violence also affected the Kashmir region. When India gained its independence, the leader of Kashmir decided to join India instead of Pakistan. Some Kashmiris (kash-MIR-eez) wanted to have their own nation, while the Pakistani government thought that Kashmir should belong to Pakistan. Violent fighting broke out between Indian and Pakistani soldiers. In 1949, the United Nations negotiated a *cease-fire,* or truce, and divided the territory between India and Pakistan.

A Free India

In 1950, India became a *socialist* democratic republic. This meant the government would own and control most industries, but representatives from each state and territory would be elected to *Parliament* (PAR-luh-munt), the legislative group that makes the laws.

Prime Minister Nehru tried to steer India into the modern world. He began to build businesses and factories in the country. Many of the prime ministers who came after Nehru have worked to bring India into the technological age. One of them was Nehru's daughter, Indira Gandhi (no relation to Mohandas Gandhi), who served as prime minister of India from 1967 until 1977 and from 1980 to 1984. During this time she implemented land reform policies and helped the Bengali people establish an independent country out of part of eastern India, now called Bangladesh. But Gandhi also resorted to increasingly repressive measures as civil unrest grew in the early 1970s, the result of food shortages and inflation.

In the early 1980s, a group of Sikhs, believers in a religion founded in the sixteenth century, wanted to form an independent state in the Punjab region in northwestern India. After two years of violent attacks against the government, Gandhi sent Indian troops to the Punjab in 1984. The Indian Army launched an assault against a radical group of Sikhs who took over an important Sikh temple, using it as their fortress. Sikhs everywhere were outraged at the results: nearly all of the temple buildings were damaged, and hundreds of people were killed. Unrest between Sikhs and Hindus grew. Within months, Indira Gandhi was assassinated by one of her Sikh bodyguards.

India Today

The current prime minister, Atal Bihari Vajpayee, and the president, Abdul Kalam, elected in 1998 and 1997, respectively, have continued modernizing India. Poverty and population growth are slowly decreasing. Special programs are introducing new industry and farming methods. Policies promoting schools and public health have led to a rise in education levels and a drop in the birth rate. Since 1991, the economy has been growing.

However, India faces many problems. Differences in religion, caste, and language are just a few of the problems that this diverse society must deal with. Tensions between Hindus and Muslims within India have escalated, while Sikhs in the Punjab region continue their fight for an independent state.

There is also an increase in tensions between India and Pakistan, especially along the Kashmir border. Both India and Pakistan have nuclear weapons and have declared that they are willing to use them against each other. The war against *terrorists* in nearby Afghanistan that began in 2001 has complicated the situation. India's leaders worry that the alliance of Pakistan with the United States in the war against terrorism will result in a loss of support from the United States in India's stand against Pakistan.

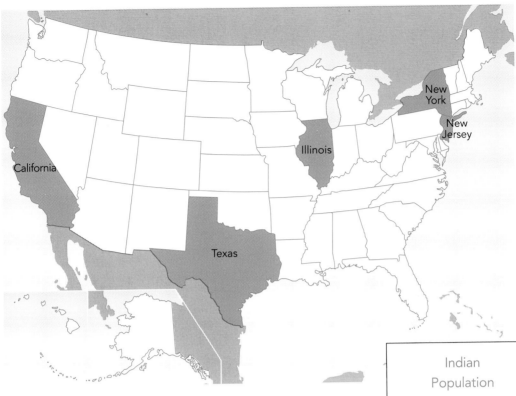

Indian Population in the U.S.	
California	359,773
New York	274,622
New Jersey	166,844
Texas	148,681
Illinois	121,767

Source: U.S. Census, 2000

Coming to America

The earliest immigrants from India arrived in California around 1900. Most were single men from the rural Punjab region in northwest India who were searching for better opportunities. They arrived in the United States at a time when public opinion had begun to turn against Asian immigrants.

As competition for jobs and land intensified, *nativist* groups such as the Asian Exclusion League blamed a growing Asian population. They pressured employers not to hire Indian and Asian immigrants. Riots and violent attacks on immigrants took place. The nativist groups also pressured Congress and the INS to restrict immigration from Asian countries. They were ultimately successful. By 1917, all Asian immigration was tightly restricted.

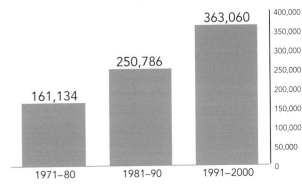

U.S./Indian Immigration by Decade

	1971–80	1981–90	1991–2000
	161,134	250,786	363,060

Source: Statistical Yearbook of the Immigration and Naturalization Service

Did you know?

Did you know that pajamas were first worn in India? When the British ruled India, they noticed people wearing comfortable, loose cotton clothing. The British wanted to imitate the style. However, they thought that pajamas were not dressy enough for day wear, so they decided to wear them to sleep in. *Pa jama* means "loose pants" in Hindi.

Even though most of the early immigrants were Sikhs, they were grouped together and called "Hindus" by immigration officials. This was due to ignorance on the part of the officials and the language barrier. In their first years in California, the immigrants worked on railroads, in agriculture, and in the lumber industry. They were instrumental in starting and supporting rice farming in California. Some moved on to other states, including Texas, Arizona, New Mexico, and Colorado.

Not all of the early immigrants were laborers. Some Indians came to the United States to further their education, studying at colleges and universities throughout America. Most, however, attended college on the west coast.

Over time, American attitudes toward Indians changed. Many of the early immigrants became prosperous farmers and business owners. They lobbied Congress for the right to become naturalized citizens of the United States. In 1946, the Luce-Cellar Act permitted Indians and Filipinos to become naturalized citizens of the United States. It also allowed 100 Indian immigrants into the United States each year. The Punjabis could now become citizens and sponsor family members in India to come to America.

The Bellingham Riots

One of the worst of the attacks against early Indian immigrants took place in Bellingham, Washington, on September 5, 1907. A mob of over 500 men dragged Indian immigrants from the bunkhouses where they lived, then robbed and beat them. Then they burned the bunkhouses. The Indians, many of them Sikhs, lost their savings and belongings in the riots. With no protection from the police and no jobs left (their employers had been threatened by the mob as well), the Indians left Bellingham. Some went to Everett, Washington, a nearby town. On November 5, an angry mob chased the Indians from that town as well. The Indians moved on, looking for work in California, Arizona, New Mexico, Colorado, and Texas.

The Punjabi pioneers and their children and grandchildren found they had little in common with those in the second great *migration* from India. After so much time in the United States, they felt more American than Indian.

The Second Wave

The 1965 Immigration and Naturalization Act eliminated the historical restrictions on Asian migration. Indians with technical skills, education, or family members in the United States could emigrate much more easily. As a result, many urban, highly educated Indians migrated as families.

In the 1990s, India ranked third among Asian countries sending immigrants to America. Many are employed as scientists, engineers, and doctors. They live mainly in urban areas, with about 70 percent in eight major industrial states: New York, California, New Jersey, Texas, Pennsylvania, Michigan, Illinois, and Ohio.

Life in America

This Muslim Indian young woman and her twenty-month-old niece live with their extended family in Little Rock, Arkansas. Their family has maintained many of its traditional values and customs while living in a part of the country where Indians and Muslims form a very small minority.

I ndian immigrants today come from different regions in India, speak different languages, and practice different religions. But they have created their own support system, in part through large family networks. These networks help them maintain their Indian culture within the larger American culture. But even as they strive to keep their Indian heritage alive, the new immigrants are putting down roots, gaining political power, and becoming "American."

Family

In America, Indians continue their commitment to a stable family life, which often includes extended families. Parents pay close attention to their children. Children are encouraged to work hard and make their parents proud of them.

Traditionally, marriages were arranged, a custom that is still followed by many Indians today. However, Indian Americans feel freer to say no to a match if it doesn't please them. The Indian tradition that the man is the head of the household and the American idea of equality of the sexes cause conflict for some Indian American families. In spite of this, Indians have the highest marriage rate with the fewest separations and divorces of any immigrant group in America.

Work

As the most highly educated immigrant group in America, it is no surprise that Indians also have the highest household income. Indians are well represented in America's health care and technical professions. There are also many Indian entrepreneurs, people who have started their own businesses.

Traditionally, Indian women have been wives and mothers and have stayed at home with their children. But many Indian American women have careers or jobs outside the home.

Did you know?

Indian immigrants are among the most well educated and prosperous in America. About 89 percent have completed high school, 65 percent have completed college, and 40 percent hold an advanced degree. As a group, their income is higher than that of any other foreign-born group in the United States.

School

Indian parents expect their children to work hard and excel in school. Some first-generation immigrant students have trouble fitting in at school. Many, even though they know English, enroll in English as a second language (ESL) classes when they first arrive in America. Because of the differences between British and American English, everyday language may be confusing.

Indian American students are often teased for their accent, their dress, and their commitment to education. They also have to adjust their behavior in class. In America, teachers expect students to participate in class by asking questions and discussing topics. In contrast, Indian teachers lecture while students quietly take notes.

In America, students find more freedom to follow their own interests and to choose the college they want to attend.

Religion

Religion is very important to most Indians and Indian Americans. It is also the source of tension between the many *ethnic groups*. Most Indians are Hindu, but there are also many Muslims. Christians, Sikhs, Buddhists, and Jains together make up nearly 7 percent of the population.

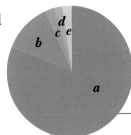

India's
Religious Groups

a	Hindu	81.3%
b	Muslim	12%
c	Christian	2.3%
d	Sikh	1.9%
e	Other	2.5%

Source: CIA World Factbook, *2002*

Members of the Hindu Temple Vraj in Schuylkill Haven, Pennsylvania, gather for a service in the temple's main hall. The ornate sandstone temple stands amid fields in the rolling farmland of Pennsylvania's Amish country.

Indian American Hindus say that their Hindu traditions and community are very important to them. Their religion reinforces Indian traditions within the American society. Beliefs about proper dress, dating and marriage customs, and family importance are influenced and strengthened by Hindu community worship and celebrations.

About 4 million Indians belong to the Church of St. Thomas, an Orthodox Church that is believed to have been established by one of Christ's disciples. Because Orthodox Christians also migrated from Syria into India, Orthodox Christians are sometimes called Syrian Christians. There are also many Protestant Christians in India.

Although few Indians practice Buddhism today, the religion got its start in India in the fifth century B.C. It spread throughout Asia, including China, Cambodia, Laos, Korea, and Japan.

Hinduism

Hinduism began in India about 1500 B.C. It has influenced other major world religions and has been influenced by them in return.

Although Hindus in one region may not share many beliefs with those in a distant area, there are some beliefs that are common to all Hindus. Hindus believe that a person's good or bad deeds are rewarded or punished in the life after death. This belief is called *karma*.

The four Vedas (VAY-duhs or VEE-duhs) are the holy writings of Hinduism. The four books of the Veda are used primarily by Hindu priests. Hinduism also includes stories that teach about the Hindu gods and values.

Holidays and Festivals

Many of the holidays celebrated by Indians in America are related to their Hindu or Muslim faith.

The Hindu calendar is based in part on the lunar cycle. This means that the dates of Hindu festivals change from year to year. Diwali and Holi are two of the Hindu festivals that are celebrated in Indian American communities.

Diwali is the Hindu New Year. This "festival of lights" comes at the end of October or the beginning of November, at the darkest time of the month, and lasts five days. For some Hindus, it is a holy celebration, filled with rituals. Others see it mostly as a time for socializing and exchanging gifts. In America, celebrations usually take the form of a community festival with dances and traditional art exhibits, followed the next day by celebrations at home. Hindu Americans decorate their homes and place lights, lamps, or candles in windows and on sidewalks and rooftops to attract Lakshmi, the goddess of wealth. Foods and prayers are offered to the gods. Then everyone gathers for a feast of traditional holiday foods. Because Diwali celebrates renewal, most Indians wear new clothes for the holiday and give and receive presents. Adults teach children how to make *rangoli* designs from colored flour on the floor. The designs invite wealth and good health into the home.

Holi is another Hindu festival. Held in February or March, it celebrates the coming of spring. At celebrations and feasts in America, people splash each other with brightly colored water and powder to scare away evil spirits.

Diwali and Holi are also celebrated by Sikhs, but the holidays have a slightly different meaning. During Diwali, Sikhs celebrate the life of a famous military and religious leader, Guru Hargobind. After Holi, Sikhs have a spring festival called Hola Mahalla. During this festival, they act out legends from their history. In America, these storytelling and acting performances reinforce a connection to Sikh roots and traditions.

Indian Muslims in America observe the holy month of Ramadan, fasting and praying each day. Then they celebrate Eid al-Fitr, the feast that marks the end of Ramadan. This is a time for friends and family to gather and exchange gifts. Other traditional Islamic holidays are also celebrated.

More than 2,000 Sikhs march in their traditional dress during the fourth annual Hola Mahalla Parade on March 24, 2002, in Livingston, California. The event celebrates the 300th birthday of the Siri Guru Granth Sahib or Sikh holy book.

Two young performers dance with the Hindu Temple Rhythms dance group at the Detroit Historical Museum during the Indian Cultural Workshop in 2001. The workshop featured traditional Hindu dances and introduced many residents of Michigan to the culture of India and the Hindu religion.

The Arts

Indian Americans are on the cutting edge of the arts in many communities across the United States. India is well known for its cloth art, rugs, painting, music, sculpture, and movie industry. Indian Americans are building on this rich heritage.

Many young Indian immigrants and second-generation Indian Americans are joining the entertainment and media industries in the United States. They see film as a way to powerfully express their two cultures. Indian American women, especially, feel that filmmaking gives voice to a previously silent part of the Indian community. Mira Nair, director of the acclaimed film *Monsoon Wedding*, divides her time between America and India. Her new film, *Hysterical Blindness*, stars American actors, Uma Thurman and Gena Rowlands.

Traditional Indian music and dance attract many Indian Americans. For example, classes held in the San Francisco Bay area introduce students to classical sixteenth-century northern Indian music. In Cleveland, Ohio, an annual four-day music festival celebrating the works of Thyagaraja, an eighteenth-century Indian composer, draws over 3,000 attendees each day.

Spotlight on
Zubin Mehta

Zubin Mehta has been conducting symphony orchestras since 1958. Born in 1939, in Bombay, India, he grew up around music and musicians. Mehta first appeared in the United States when he conducted the Philadelphia Symphony Orchestra in 1960. He has also served as music director for the Los Angeles and New York Philharmonics. In 1994, he staged a concert in India with the Israel Philharmonic Orchestra, opening political doors between India and Israel that had been closed for thirty years.

Food

Indian immigrants introduced their foods to Americans long ago. Most Indian restaurants in America serve foods typical of northern India, although foods from other regions are starting to appear on menus as well. With its emphasis on vegetables, legumes, and grains, Indian cooking attracts the attention of many vegetarians in America. In parts of California and Arizona, dishes such as chicken curry with jalapeño peppers and enchiladas reflect the blending of cultures that occurred when early Punjabi immigrants married Mexican women.

India's spices reached American shores even earlier. Since ancient

Did you know?

India is not only a country; it is also a subcontinent. This means it is a large landmass that is politically separate from the continent of Asia even though it is part of the continent. In fact, India takes up most of southern Asia. The tip of India juts out into the Indian Ocean.

times, traders have traveled to India in search of pepper, cinnamon, cardamom, and other spices. In fact, Christopher Columbus was searching for a new trade route to India when he discovered the Americas.

Wheat, rice, and lentils are important to the Indian diet. A wheat bread called chapati is served with most meals. Basmati rice, which has a nutty flavor, is often served as a side dish. Lentils are cooked in a stew called *daal*.

Tandoori cooking is popular in northern India. Pieces of meat, chicken, or lamb are put on long sticks and cooked over the fire in a tandoor, a clay oven. Bread cooked in a tandoor oven is called naan or roti. Two favorite desserts from this region are spiced rice pudding and *kulfi*, an ice cream.

Recipe

Chemeen Thoren (Stir-Fried Shrimp with Coconut)

This recipe comes from southern India, where the miles of coastline yield huge harvests of shrimp. The curry leaves that are used in this recipe come from the curry tree, a citrus tree native to India. The British invented curry powder—which has no curry leaves in it—in an effort to duplicate the flavors of Indian cooking. You may be able to find fresh curry leaves in an Asian market.

3/4 cup grated unsweetened coconut

2 cloves garlic, crushed

1 fresh green chili (serrano or Thai), split lengthwise

3/4 to 1 teaspoon salt

Ground masala:

    1 teaspoon coriander

    1/4 teaspoon cayenne

    1/4 teaspoon turmeric

3 tablespoons vegetable oil

1 teaspoon mustard seeds

2 dried red chilies

10 fresh curry leaves

1-1/2 pounds shrimp, shelled and deveined, cut into 1/4-inch pieces

Combine the coconut, garlic, green chili, salt, and ground masala in a bowl with about 1/4 cup of water to make a moist ball. Set aside.

In a wok, heat the oil over medium heat. Add the mustard seeds and cover. When the seeds have popped, toss in the red chilies and curry leaves. After the leaves crackle for a few seconds, put in the shrimp and stir-fry for one minute. Stir in the coconut mixture and continue frying for another 3 minutes or until the shrimp are just cooked through.

Serves 6.

Source: Adapted from Savoring the Spice Coast of India: Fresh Flavors from Kerala *by Maya Kaimal*

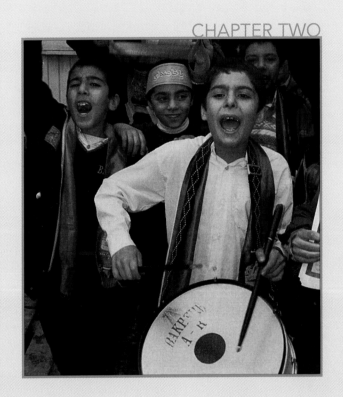

CHAPTER TWO

Iranians

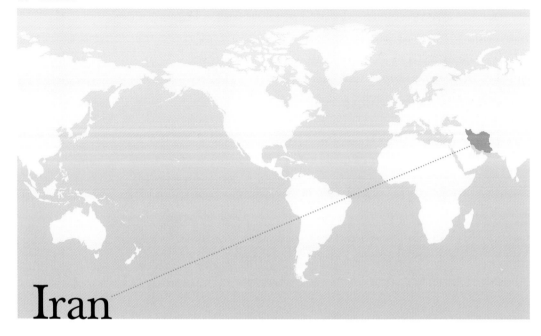

Iran

is the modern name of the ancient kingdom of Persia (PUR-zhuh). The name "Iran" (ih-RAN) is short for *Aryanem,* "Land of the Aryans." These Indo-European Aryan people had migrated from the steppes of Russia. Some of them moved into northern Europe. Other tribes moved south into Asia and established the Persian Empire. For over a hundred years, the Persian Empire, extending into India, was the largest and most powerful *empire* in the world.

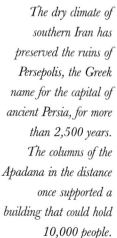

The dry climate of southern Iran has preserved the ruins of Persepolis, the Greek name for the capital of ancient Persia, for more than 2,500 years. The columns of the Apadana in the distance once supported a building that could hold 10,000 people.

In the seventh century, Islamic Arabs invaded Persia and converted most of its people to Islam. The common religion of Islam binds Iran to its Arab neighbors, but only a few Iranians are Arabs. Instead, about half of all Iranians are Persians. The next largest group is the Azeri Turks, who live in northwestern Iran near Turkey and are ethnically related to the Turkish. The Kurds, a nomadic Indo-European group made up of many tribes, live in the mountains of western and northern Iran. They are Sunni (SOO-nee) Muslims, as opposed to the majority of Muslims in Iran, who are Shi'ite (SHE-ite) Muslims. Religious differences, as well as the Kurds' desire for an independent nation, have caused much tension between the Iranian government and the Kurds. There are also many other, smaller *ethnic groups* in Iran.

A Quick Look Back

The Persian Empire, one of the greatest of the early *civilizations,* once included what is now Iran, Iraq, Palestine, Syria, and Asia Minor. Literature, music, art, rug-making, architecture, and science flourished in Persia at a time when some civilizations had no written language or organized government.

During the nineteenth century, Russia and Britain tried to influence Iran's politics and *economy* because of its important location. Russia wanted Iran's access to ports on the Caspian Sea. Britain was worried about being cut off from India, an important part of its empire. But, by the late 1800s, many Iranians resented the control that foreign countries seemed to have over their shah, or king. They demanded a constitutional government. In 1906, the shah agreed to an elected legislature called a parliament and a *constitution* that outlined the responsibilities of each government group.

Even with constitutional reform, Russia and Britain continued to influence Iran's government. The British had discovered and developed oil wells in Iran and wanted to protect these valuable assets. The outbreak of World War I in 1914 worsened Iran's suffering economy. Although Iran did not take a side during the war, many battles were fought in the country. Several key supply routes to the Persian Gulf, the Arabian Sea, and the Caspian Sea crossed and passed through Iran. British oil reserves were in the region. As the war expanded into Africa,

Iran became a staging ground for troops and supplies. Whole villages in Iran were destroyed, and food became very scarce. Starvation probably killed more Iranians than the war itself.

Modernizing Iran

In 1921, with British support, Reza Khan took power in Iran. He crowned himself shah of a new Pahlavi *dynasty* in 1926 and officially changed the country's name to Iran. Reza Shah's main goal was to modernize Iran through industrialization and development of a public education system. Knowing that education was necessary for his programs to be successful, Reza Shah encouraged Iranians to continue their education in Britain and the United States. A national banking system was established, as well as a cross-country railroad. Rules promoting equality for women were instituted, including the right not to wear a veil, or *chador,* as required by Islamic law. Although these changes improved the lives of many Iranians, there was widespread resentment at Reza Shah's *dictatorial* approach.

World War II

World War II interrupted many of Reza Shah's programs. Although Iran declared itself a neutral country, its oil resources and key location were too valuable for the Allies to ignore. Allied British and Soviet Russian troops invaded Iran in 1941, taking control of the railroad and oil reserves. Reza Shah was *exiled,* forced to leave Iran. His son, Mohammad Reza Shah, was allowed to rule Iran with the understanding that he would rule according to the constitution, instead of as the dictator his father had been.

Mohammed Reza Shah, who became known simply as the shah, struggled after World War II. Many Iranians wanted the government to take control of the British-owned oil company in southwestern Iran. Mohammad Mosaddeq, a member of the Iranian parliament, became the leader of the movement to nationalize the oil industry. In 1951, the Iranian parliament took control of the oil company and appointed Mosaddeq prime minister. This action stripped the shah of his power to lead the country.

Britain responded by blocking all sales of Iran's oil. The United States tried to negotiate a compromise between the two countries without success. The United States began to fear that the Soviet Union would try to take over Iran. The U.S. Central Intelligence Agency worked with the shah's supporters to overthrow Mosaddeq in 1953. Once the shah was back in power, he allowed European and U.S. interests to take over the oil company once again.

The shah of Iran (right), dressed in a military uniform, meets with President Harry Truman in Washington, D.C., in 1949. U.S. support for the shah's government was one factor that led to his overthrow by religious fundamentalists in 1979.

The shah's rule became increasingly authoritarian after 1953. He created a secret police force to silence any opposition. His government's strong relationship with the United States led many Iranians to distrust the shah. In the early 1960s, the Islamic clergy, especially Ayatollah Ruholla Khomeini (*eye*-yuh-TOL-uh Ko-MAY-nee), criticized the shah's actions. (*Ayatollah* is a title used by Shi'ite Muslims to refer to religious leaders.) Nonreligious Iranians also opposed the shah. They wanted the government to be more democratic. By the late 1970s, these two groups were united in their call for a new government.

Ayatollah Khomeini

In January 1979, the shah knew he had lost control of Iran and left the country. Ayatollah Khomeini, the religious leader, took over the country two weeks later. He declared Iran to be an Islamic republic. He represented those in the country who wanted to see Iran return to a religious strictness and rid itself of all Western ideas. Under this new *regime,* women again had to veil themselves in the *chador* and could go out in public only in the company of a male family member. People were punished, persecuted, or put to death if they broke strict Islamic laws. Believers in the Baha'i faith were driven out of Iran or killed.

Ruholla Khomeini became known as Ayatollah Khomeini. Ayatollah is a term for a Shi'ite scholar and religious leader. It literally means "gift of God."

Many people left Iran during this time, especially those in the middle and upper classes. Some had supported the shah. Others were concerned about the growing violence against anything modern. A depressed world economy caused the cost of food and goods to rise. Unemployment went up, too. The Kurds and other small ethnic groups in northwest Iran began rioting and demanding freedom.

In November 1979, Iranian students, protesting against the shah's being allowed to live in the United States, broke into the U.S. embassy in Tehran (teh-RAN), the capital of Iran. They took sixty-six Americans *hostage,* demanding that the

United States return the shah to Iran to stand trial for crimes that he may have committed. Tensions between Iran and the United States grew as the days ticked by. The hostages were kept in horrible conditions until their eventual release fifteen months later.

A border dispute between Iran and Iraq (ih-RAK) escalated into the Iran-Iraq War when Iraqi troops invaded Iran in 1980. But religious differences were also behind the attack. Iraq was afraid that Iran's Islamic government would encourage Shi'ite Muslims in Iraq to rebel. Iraq's president, Saddam Hussein, expected an easy victory over a weakened Iran. But the Iranians fought hard to defend their country. The war lasted eight years. Over 100,000 lives were lost. Both countries went into debt because of the war's high cost.

Iran Today

In 1989, Iran instituted a presidential office. The president is the head of the executive branch and carries out policies determined by the ayatollah, or spiritual leader. An Islamic legislative body makes the laws.

President Ali Akbar Hashemi Rafsanjani was elected in 1989 and began to soften some of the policies that Ayatollah Khomeini had enforced. When Mohammed Khatami was elected president in 1997, he continued to support more freedom of expression. Through most of the 1990s, the United States imposed economic *sanctions* against Iran to protest its suspected links with *terrorists*. Iran made friendly gestures toward the United States while secretly funding anti-American groups. Following Khatami's election, however, the two countries began to develop a better relationship.

After suffering from losses in the Iran-Iraq War, Iran is beginning to show signs of economic recovery. It is rich in oil and natural gas and has become self-sufficient in growing its own food.

Unrest between the different ethnic and religious groups still troubles Iran. Many of the smaller ethnic groups, including the Kurds and Arabs, hoped the revolution would improve their position in Iran. But, in fact, the opposite has happened. They have even less representation in the current government than they had before. As a result, protests and violence break out frequently in different parts of Iran.

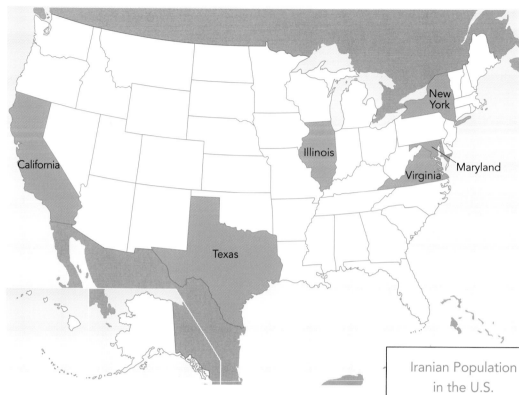

New York

Illinois

California

Virginia

Maryland

Texas

Iranian Population in the U.S.	
California	152,870
Maryland	23,442
Texas	22,153
New York	18,025
Virginia	17,132
Illinois	11,573

Source: U.S. Census, 2000

Coming to America

I t is hard to know how many immigrants came to the United States from Iran before 1924, but the number is probably only a few hundred. Because Iran was located in the same part of the world as the Turkish Ottoman Empire, immigration officials often labeled anyone from that area as "Turks from Asia." Many of the early immigrants were actually Persian-Iranian Christians and Muslims who traveled through Syria to the Mediterranean Sea, where they took steamships to the United States and Canada.

Some of the early Iranian immigrants left their homeland to escape being drafted into the Turkish army. Originally farmers and craftspeople, the new immigrants became

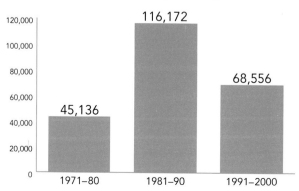

U.S./Iranian Immigration by Decade

116,172

120,000

100,000

80,000

68,556

60,000

45,136

40,000

20,000

0

1971–80   1981–90   1991–2000

Source: Statistical Yearbook of the Immigration and Naturalization Service

traveling peddlers, selling merchandise door-to-door. Most intended to stay in America only a short time. But, because of their success, they stayed permanently. They invested the money they earned from their traveling sales into dry goods stores and other small businesses.

In 1924, the U.S. Congress passed legislation that limited immigration from Iran to only 100 immigrants per year. After World War II, however, many wealthy Iranians sent their children, mainly sons, to attend universities and colleges in the United States. Some of these students stayed in America and later became citizens.

The 1965 Immigration and Naturalization Act made it easier for Iranians to come to the United States. Many well-educated Iranians with established professions came to the United States after 1965.

Many of the Iranians who came for higher education stayed in the United States and opened small businesses. Some opened restaurants. Others opened carpet outlets, tapping into the enormous supply of traditionally woven and hand-dyed rugs in Iran. These mostly young, first-generation Iranians applied for citizenship and became a part of the fabric of American life. They established family *networks* and used the new immigration laws to sponsor family members to come to the United States.

More Iranian immigrants came to the United States during the 1980s than in any other decade. Some were supporters of the deposed shah and opposed Ayatollah Khomeni's leadership and religious strictness. Many immigrants fled Iran to escape the torture and death that awaited them if they were caught practicing a religion other than Islam. Many others came to escape the destruction and the poverty caused by the Iran-Iraq War.

Since 1989, the new government of Iran has relaxed some of the restrictions against free speech. The economy is still slowly recovering from the costly war with Iraq. But even though conditions have improved for most Persian Iranians, members of some minority groups, such as the Azerbaijani, Kurds, and Baluchis, have immigrated to escape persecution from both the Iranian and Iraqi governments because of their ethnic group or religion. Young Iranians chafe at the narrowness of the lifestyle available to them. People from these groups make up the most recent wave of Iranians seeking protection and freedom in the United States.

Spotlight on
AZADEH TABAZADEH

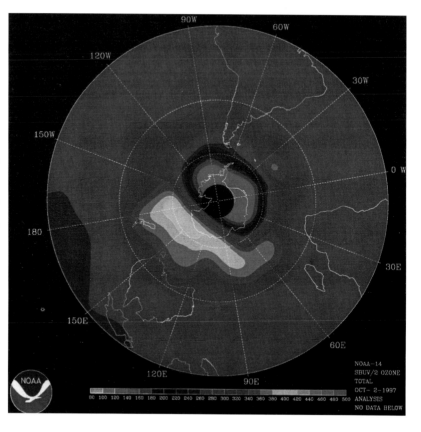

This computer-enhanced photograph of the South Pole from the National Oceanic and Atmospheric Administration shows a large light-colored area where the ozone layer has been damaged. Iranian immigrant Azadeh Tabazadeh demonstrated that this damage was caused by human-made chemicals in the atmosphere.

One of the most highly regarded scientists in America today escaped from Iran at the age of seventeen. In 1980, Ayatollah Khomeini assumed power in Iran. Suddenly women's rights were restricted. Azadeh Tabazadeh's parents agreed to help her leave the country, knowing that she would have more opportunities in America. Tabazadeh paid smugglers to take her from to Pakistan and from there *emigrated* to the United States. She attended the University of California in Los Angeles, studying chemistry.

In 1992, Tabazadeh proved that human-made chlorofluorocarbons (CFCs) were destroying the ozone layer. She was one of the first scientists to make the connection between global warming and a weakened ozone layer. In 1996, the U.S. government banned CFCs.

Today, Tabazadeh is a senior research scientist at the National Aeronautics and Space Administration (NASA) Ames Research Center in California. In 2002, she was named one of *Popular Science's* "Brilliant 10," scientists who are changing the world.

Life in America

I ranian immigrants who arrived before 1980 were, for the most part, educated and professional people seeking opportunity in the United States. Many of them had acquired some English through family business contacts in Iran. Other than a brief but intense time in the late 1970s, they easily established themselves as businesspeople and citizens. With their extended networks of family and friends, they have managed to strike a good balance between embracing the American culture and keeping their own customs and identity.

Since 1980, immigrants have had a more difficult time adjusting to American life, language, and culture. Many are from remote tribal groups. Of these people, the Kurds and the Baluchis have had the most trouble in the transition. They often left Iran as *refugees,* escaping from persecution based on their ethnic background or religion.

Family

Although clannish, Iranian Americans are known for their hospitality. They enjoy visitors to their homes and make them feel welcome. But family is at the center of Iranian social life.

Families eat together as often as possible. Working fathers and mothers try to eat lunch at home with their small children if they can. Owners of small businesses often take their babies and toddlers to work with them.

In America, many generations of an Iranian family live in one home. Other members may live nearby. In this way, Iranian families take care of one another, from childhood, to adulthood, to old age.

Most Iranian American women are well educated. But, as Muslims, the women are expected to obey their fathers, husbands, or brothers in important family matters. Many Iranian American men still send to Iran for brides. This helps ensure that the brides will be traditional, obedient, and committed to the Islamic faith. Family members in Iran still help choose suitable marriage partners for grown-up children.

Second-generation Iranian Americans have adapted well to American life. The closeness of the family unit seems to protect Iranian American teenagers from the typical distance between adolescents and their elders. Grandparents, however, complain that some customs are being lost and that the fast pace of American life and the demands of work make many parents and children shortchange family time. Traditional tea and coffee visits with grandparents and prayer time at the mosque are neglected under the demands of school and extracurricular activities.

Iranian American women experience a greater freedom in the United States as Iranian families become more Westernized. They are more willing to set their own course without the endorsement of a male family member.

Did you know?

A favorite game of Iranians is chess. Iranians say that chess was invented by the Persians more than 2,000 years ago. Today, it is played in many Iranian American homes, with fathers teaching their sons and daughters the rules and moves of the game.

Work

Since 1980, many Kurds, Baluchis, and members of other remote tribal groups have come to the United States as refugees. Some have had to go on welfare because they have not been able to find jobs. Others get low-wage work that does not pay them enough to support their families.

Most of the earlier immigrants and their families are well established in the American workplace. Many are professionals: doctors, lawyers, architects, and accountants. Others, especially Iranians of Persian or Armenian descent, have established family networks that have helped them start groceries, restaurants, and other small, service-related businesses. For those who are self-employed, the working day is usually ten hours a day or longer. Although their children often spend time at the workplace, these long hours detract from the time many would like to spend with their elders and children or at religious ceremonies.

School

Iranian families expect their children to do well in school. Many sacrifices are made within the family to provide the possibility of college for the children. Persian, Armenian, and Syrian Iranians seem to adapt fairly easily to American elementary and secondary schools. Many of them already speak English and one or two other languages.

Kurds, Baluchi, and other tribal Iranians usually spend time in ESL classes when they first start school in the United States. Because they grew up in tribes in rural areas without electricity, these young Iranians lack exposure to American culture through television and movies, so they experience culture shock as a result.

Religion

Almost all Iranian Americans are Muslim—about 98 percent. About 95 percent of Iranian Americans are Shi'ite Muslims; the other 3 percent are Sunni.

On Friday, the Muslim day of worship, Iranian American families gather at the mosque for the weekly prayer service. Before entering, they remove their shoes and wash their hands, faces, and feet in a fountain of running water. Inside the mosque, Persian carpets cover the floor. Tiles decorate the walls and floors, too. They are covered with writings from the Muslim holy book, the Qur'an (Koran).

Tiny groups of Jews, Armenian Christians, Zoroastrians (ZOH-rast-tree-ahnz), and Baha'is make up the remaining small percentage of Iranian Americans who follow other beliefs.

Zoroastrianism is an ancient Persian religion. It was the official religion of Persia before the spread of Islam in the seventh century. Followers of this religion believe in a supreme god and in the struggle in this world between good spirits—represented by fire—and bad spirits—represented by darkness.

A Muslim faces east toward Mecca at a mosque near Abiquiu, New Mexico. The mosque is part of Dar al Islam, a nonprofit organization that teaches non-Muslims about Islam.

The Baha'i (bah-HIGH) religion grew out of Islam. *(Refer to* The Newest Americans A–D, *pages 33–34 for more information about Islam.)* It was founded by Bahaullah, a Muslim holy man, in the 1860s. Baha'i teaches that all people belong to one global family and that barriers of race, gender, religion, and nation must be broken down.

Other Iranian American celebrations are related to Islam. The Islamic observances of Ramadan, Eid al-Fitr, and Ashura are important days in the Iranian year. Some Iranian families also celebrate American holidays such as Thanksgiving.

An Ancient Art

Persian carpet weaving dates back thousands of years. Beautiful woven carpets have always been used for prayer. They have also been used as furniture, doors, camels' saddle blankets, and for sitting and sleeping. Ancient Persian carpets dating back as far as 500 B.C. have been discovered.

Carpet weaving requires a lot of skill and labor. It may take three years to weave one carpet by hand. One square yard (0.8 square meter) of carpet can have 1 million hand-tied knots. A skilled worker can tie 12,000 knots per day.

Girls are taught at a young age how to weave the Persian designs into rugs.

They also learn about the natural dyes and their meaning. The best dyes come from rose petals, pistachio and walnut shells, and leaves. The color red means happiness and riches. Blue wards off the evil eye or bad spirits. Orange represents faith. White is seldom used because it represents grief. Green is a sacred color, associated with the Prophet Mohammad, and is rarely used.

Many Iranian immigrants to the United States have started Persian carpet outlets. Because of their family connections to weavers back in Iran, these Iranian Americans are able to import carpets to sell. Persian carpets are popular all over the world.

The Arts

The ancient Persians' love of beauty has been handed down to their *descendants*. Perhaps because the desert is a part of their heritage, Iranians admire formal gardens. They may have been the first people to grow roses in gardens. In America, as in their homeland, many Iranians have created gardens that are works of art.

Iranian Americans have a special connection to the textile arts. Iranian carpet weavers have long been considered the best in the world. Persian carpet designs differ, depending on which ethnic group makes them. Kurdish carpets are filled with animal designs, while carpets from Baluchistan often have the tree of life in the center.

Iranian miniatures, or small paintings on glass or paper, are tiny masterpieces. Strict Islamic beliefs do not allow artists to show the human form, so many miniatures are landscapes filled with gardens and animal life. This fascination with miniature art has traveled to America with Iranian immigrants.

Food

Persian cooking traditions spread throughout the Middle East as the Persian Empire expanded. Many of these foods have been handed down through the generations, as have the Iranian customs of hospitality. These customs and menus have traveled to America, too. Most Iranian American restaurant owners serve American dishes. But the menus also offer kabobs, vegetables and meat cooked and served on a skewer or stick, and fluffy rice.

Food is a great bond and tradition for Iranian Americans. Long-grained, fluffy rice called *chelo* is served at almost every meal. It is mixed with fruit, vegetables, and meat. The only food most Iranians do not eat is pork, which is taboo for Muslims. *Chelo* kabob, meat and rice together, is Iran's national dish and a favorite dish for Iranian Americans. Some American foods like jalapeños and tortillas have found their way into Iranian American homes. The spiciness of the

Tea, Anyone?

Tea is a favorite drink in Iran. Leisure time with family and friends is spent drinking tea and talking about world and family events. A small glass of tea is the first thing offered to a visitor in an Iranian home.

Tea is served from a copper urn called a samovar. Plenty of sugar is added, but nothing else. When they picnic, traditional Iranians sometimes take a tea samovar with them.

peppers and the flat bread of the flour tortillas are similar to some Iranian foods.

An Iranian American dinner will have many side dishes. Fresh parsley, chives, dill, tarragon, mint, and red radishes, with feta cheese and walnuts, may top these sides. Bread is a mainstay of the Iranian diet. Although many homemakers still make their own bread, most Iranian Americans buy their bread at local Iranian American delis and specialty stores.

Recipe

Mahi-ye sir-dagh ba narenj (Garlic and Seville Orange Fish)

4 fish fillets (about 2 pounds, 1/2 inch thick), preferably red snapper, orange roughy, or sea bass

2 tablespoons all-purpose flour

2 teaspoons salt

4 tablespoons vegetable oil, butter, or ghee (clarified butter)

10 cloves garlic, peeled

1/2 teaspoon ground turmeric or saffron threads

1 teaspoon freshly ground black pepper

1/2 cup fish broth or water

1 cup Seville orange juice, or a mixture of 1/2 cup fresh orange juice and 1/4 cup of lime juice.

Wash the fish and pat dry. Mix 1 tablespoon of the flour and 1 teaspoon salt. Dust both sides of the fillets with the flour mixture.

In a large skillet, heat 2 tablespoons oil or butter over medium heat. Add the fish and sauté each side for 2 minutes. Remove from skillet and set aside.

In the same skillet, heat the remaining 2 tablespoons oil or butter over medium heat. Add the garlic and stir-fry for 5 minutes, until golden brown. Add the turmeric, remaining salt, and the pepper. Stir-fry 1 minute longer, then add the fish broth.

Dissolve the remaining tablespoon of flour in the orange juice and add to the skillet. Bring to a boil, remove from heat, and season to taste.

Just prior to serving, add the fish to the orange juice mixture in the skillet and simmer for 2 minutes, until the fish is tender. To serve, place the fish on a platter and garnish with fresh herbs and scallions. Pour the sauce over it and serve with rice. Serves 4.

Source: Taste of Persia: An Introduction to Persian Cooking *by Najmieh Batmanglij*

CHAPTER THREE

Iraqis

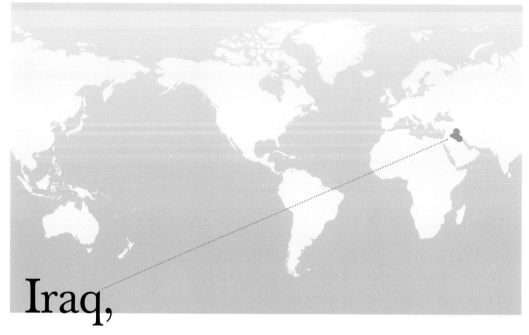

Iraq,

located in southwestern Asia, the center of the Middle East, is a little larger than the state of California. Most Iraqis are of Arab descent. The Kurds are the largest minority group, scattered in tribal units throughout northern Iraq and neighboring Iran. But there are also Iraqis of Turkish and Persian descent in Iraq. Nearly everyone in Iraq is Muslim.

A Quick Look Back

Many great cultures have risen and fallen on Iraqi soil, including the Sumerian, Babylonian, Assyrian, and Greek civilizations. In 650 A.D., followers of the Prophet Mohammad invaded Iraq and converted the people to Islam.

Turkish troops invaded Iraq in the early 1500s. Iraq became part of the Ottoman Empire and remained under its control for nearly 400 years.

Independence

With the Allies' victory in World War I, the Ottoman Empire was divided into several new nations, including Iraq. In early negotiations with the British and French, the Kurds expected that an independent Kurdistan would be one of the new countries. Instead, most of the Kurdish lands and people were divided among Iran, Iraq, Syria, and Turkey.

Iraq's
Ethnic Groups

a Arabs   79%

b Kurdish   16%

c Persian   3%

d Turkish   2%

Source: CIA
World Factbook, *2002*

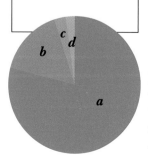

The British remained in Iraq for a decade following the end of World War I, but a provisional Iraqi government was in place by 1921. Faisal al-Husein (FIE-sahl all-hoo-SAYN), an Iraqi who had fought against the Ottoman Empire in the war, was chosen as king by the British. A council of Arab ministers (government leaders) advised the king. Britain maintained some control over the new country until 1932, when Iraq was recognized as an independent country.

Iraq served as a supply center for the Allies during much of World War II. When the war ended in 1945, Iraq faced many problems. The country was deeply in debt. Minority groups struggled to gain political power. Widespread shortages of food and goods caused hardship for many Iraqis. When Israel became an independent state in 1948, over 120,000 Iraqi Jews *emigrated* to Israel. Other Iraqis emigrated to the United States and other Western countries. This drain of educated people further hurt the Iraqi *economy*. With the explosion of the automotive industry in the West and the reconstruction of Europe after World War II, however, increased income from oil production in the early 1950s finally brought relief from Iraq's postwar poverty.

Brain Drain

When conditions in a country deteriorate, economically or politically, educated and skilled people are often the first to emigrate to other countries. This is described as a "brain drain." These creative, experienced people would normally be starting businesses, educating others, and pushing for change in government policies. With their departure, the remaining population often lacks the power or leadership to demand better government.

Revolution

In 1968, after a series of military power struggles, the Baath (bah-AHTH) Party took control of Iraq. The party's goal was to create a *socialist* government that was not ruled by religion. The government soon took control of privately owned oil companies and numerous construction projects. Many large, privately owned companies were taken over by the Iraqi government, ending any large-scale free enterprise efforts by Iraqis.

In response to unrest in Kurdish areas, the Baath Party leaders agreed to let the Kurds rule themselves in areas where they were the majority of the population. However, this was

Members of a Kurdish family walk down a mountain carrying their few belongings to a refugee camp. Thousands of Iraqi Kurds were displaced from their homes in northern Iraq following a failed rebellion against Saddam Hussein.

only an empty promise given to buy the government time. The Kurdish region in northern Iraq had the most productive oil fields, which the Iraqi government didn't want to give up.

It lasted a year until the Kurdish army finally gave up. As the war ended, the Iraqi government identified a smaller area in northern Iraq as "Kurdish." Students in schools and universities were not allowed to study the Kurdish history or language. Arab Iraqis were resettled in Kurdish areas in an effort to weaken any political power that the Kurds might have.

Saddam Hussein, a member of the Baath Party, became president of Iraq in 1979.

The Iran-Iraq War

At the same time that Saddam Hussein came to power, a power shift took place in neighboring Iran. Ayatollah Khomeini (*eye*-yuh-TOL-uh Ko-MAY-nee) overthrew the shah (king) of Iran. The government in Iran was now guided by strict Islamic laws. This new Islamic state of Iran threatened Iraq. Many Islamic *fundamentalists* wanted the same kind of religious state in Iraq. Hussein sent his troops into Iran in 1980 and began a bitter war that lasted eight years.

Hussein at first thought that Iraq would win the war quickly, gaining more territory in the Persian Gulf in the process. The former Soviet Union helped train the Iraqi army. It supported Iraq because the Ayatollah's Islamic revolution threatened to spread into Muslim areas in the Soviet Union.

Surprisingly, however, the disorganized Iranians fought back. When the Iraqi Kurds supported the Iranians, the Iraqi army retaliated by destroying many Kurdish villages. It also used chemical weapons against the Kurds and Iranians. Such weapons had not been used since World War I, when they were declared against international law. The Iraqis' disregard for international law and human rights caused outrage in the international community, beginning a long history of conflict and opposition. After hundreds of thousands of deaths, Khomeini and Hussein agreed to end the war in 1988.

The Iran-Iraq War hurt Iraq's economy. The war left the government deeply in debt, and the common people suffered. Things only got worse when, two years later, Iraq invaded another neighboring country.

The Persian Gulf War

On August 2, 1990, Iraq invaded Kuwait (koo-WAYT), its neighbor to the southeast. Iraq wanted Kuwait's wealth and access to the Persian Gulf. To justify the invasion, Saddam Hussein argued that Kuwait was part of Iraq.

The United Nations (UN) tried to convince Iraq to leave Kuwait voluntarily, but Hussein refused. In January 1991, twenty-eight nations joined together to send forces to defend Kuwait. Among the countries fighting against Iraq in the Gulf War actions, Desert Shield and Desert Storm, were the United States, Saudi Arabia, Britain, Egypt, France, Pakistan, and Syria. Within Iraq, the Kurds rebelled against the government.

Faced with this overwhelming show of force, Iraq withdrew almost immediately. It estimated that 100,000 Iraqi troops lost their lives in the Gulf War. Although the coalition discussed removing Hussein from office during the Gulf War, it ended up putting economic *sanctions,* such as a ban on selling oil, in place instead. Living conditions got so bad for the average Iraqi, however, that the UN allowed the Iraqi government to sell some oil in order to purchase food and other humanitarian supplies. Unfortunately, most of the money from the sale of oil went directly into the pockets of Hussein and his personal security force, the Republican Guard.

Iraq Today

Iraq is still ruled by Saddam Hussein and the Baath Party. He serves as president, chairman of the Revolutionary Command Council (the main decision-making body), commander of the armed forces, prime minister, and secretary-general of the Baath's Regional Command. Constitutionally, Iraq is a socialist republic, with Iraqi voters selecting their leaders. But in actual practice, Hussein rules as a dictator, appointing all representatives and controlling all aspects of the government. While Hussein and his Republican Guard get richer, the average Iraqi citizen struggles to survive. Many people who have voiced their unhappiness with the current government have been jailed or killed.

Saddam Hussein poses a threat to the stability of the region. His government has been connected to many terrorist bombings around the world. Under suspicion that his country is producing weapons of mass destruction, Hussein was ordered to submit to weapons inspections by the United Nations, or face the threat of war by the United States and coalition forces. In March 2003, when it became clear that he was not fully cooperating with UN inspectors, the United States initiated military action.

Craftspeople

In 1876, the Philadelphia Centennial Exposition celebrated America's first hundred years. It included exhibits from all over the world. The sultan of the Ottoman Empire, which included many present-day Middle Eastern countries like Iraq, sent artists and craftspeople to America for the show. They may have been the first Arabs to visit the United States. When the exhibitors returned home and told of their success, word spread throughout the Ottoman Empire that America was a land of opportunity.

Spotlight on
SADDAM HUSSEIN

President Saddam Hussein speaks to the Iraqi people during a televised address following air strikes by U.S. and British forces aimed at enforcing United Nations sanctions against Iraq following the Gulf War.

Saddam Hussein was born to a poor peasant family in 1937. Escaping the poverty of his childhood, he vowed to get ahead politically. He killed or pushed aside anyone, including family members, who got in his way.

At twenty-four years of age, Hussein attempted to kill a political rival and failed. After a two-year exile in Egypt, he returned to Iraq in 1963 and took a job as state torturer with the ruling Baath Party. By the age of thirty-two, he held the second most powerful job in Iraq. In 1979, he became president. His first act in office was to order the killings of about twenty high-ranking military officers who were political rivals. These executions of his opponents have continued throughout his reign. His attacks on the Kurds and other rebel groups have earned him the nickname "The Butcher of Baghdad."

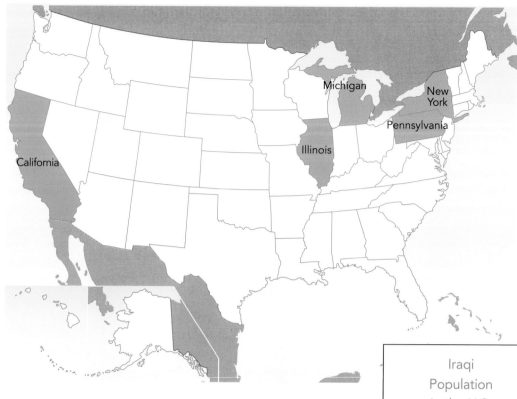

Iraqi Population in the U.S.	
Michigan	11,772
California	7,007
Pennsylvania	4,486
Illinois	2,936
New York	2,245

Source: U.S. Census, 2000

Coming to America

It is difficult to know just how many Iraqi immigrants came to America before 1924. Since Iraq was part of the Turkish Ottoman Empire, immigration officials often called everyone from that region "Turks from Asia." Other early Iraqi immigrants were recorded as "Syrians," since they often traveled to Syria before boarding ships to America. Historians believe that Iraqis made up less than 2 percent of the more than 100,000 Arabs who entered the United States before 1924.

Some early Iraqi immigrants came to America looking for economic opportunities, while others wanted to escape being drafted into the Ottoman Empire's army. Many became traveling salespeople, settling

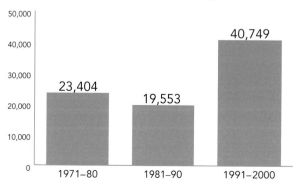

U.S./Iraqi Immigration by Decade

Source: Statistical Yearbook of the Immigration and Naturalization Service

along the railroad lines throughout America. Some worked as day laborers and factory workers in Michigan, where an Arab community, consisting mainly of Syrian Arabs, already existed. Today, Dearborn, Michigan, has one of the largest Muslim communities in the United States.

As Iraqi men and women established themselves in the United States, they sent for their families to join them. After World War I ended in 1917, many Iraqis *immigrated* because of extreme food shortages in the region. However, legislation passed in 1924 limited Iraq and other countries to 100 immigrants each year.

After World War II, Iraqis immigrated to the United States hoping for better educational and career opportunities. Many of these immigrants were educated, professional people equipped with valuable skills.

In the 1950s, the royal Iraqi government of King Faisal II emphasized improving the educational level of Iraqis. To this end, thousands of young people came to the United States for technical, financial, and managerial training. Faced with scarce employment possibilities at home, many Iraqi students decided to stay in America after completing their education.

The overthrow of King Faisal II and the takeover by the Baath Party in 1958 created turmoil in Iraq. Many middle- and upper-class Iraqis fled their troubled country. Well educated, they easily found jobs in the United States. The number of immigrants increased once again after the 1965 Immigration and Naturalization Act was passed.

The Baath Party still controls the Iraqi government, led by Saddam Hussein. Many Iraqi groups are unrepresented in the government. Any sign of *rebellion* from these groups results in severe punishment and persecution. Recent Iraqi immigrants

Controlling the Arts

The Baath government strictly controls artistic expression in Iraq. The government controls everything that appears in print or on film. Books, movies, and newspapers are all censored.

Artists and writers are careful not to anger the government. They are afraid to say anything that might upset Saddam Hussein or the Republican Guard, Hussein's personal security force. Anyone who displeases Hussein faces torture and possibly death.

As Hussein's power has grown, his image has appeared all over Iraq in huge billboard-size paintings. The evening newscasts focus on his daily activities. This publicity reminds Iraqi artists and writers that Hussein is in control. Rather than risk punishment, many simply do not publish or display their work.

to the United States include *refugees* from tribal groups like the Kurds, fleeing from torture at the hands of the Iraqi government. Other Iraqis have emigrated because of poverty.

Both the Persian Gulf War in 1991 and tensions between the United States and Saddam Hussein in 2002 have resulted in new waves of Iraqi immigrants and refugees.

Life in America

As Muslims, most Iraqi immigrants have had to adjust to America's more permissive society. Recent refugees, many of whom are from remote rural areas, face even greater challenges as they settle into their new lives in America. One of the biggest is learning to trust the police and other authority figures after a lifetime of fearing them.

Family

In America, Iraqi family members make every attempt to live near each other. In this way, traditional values and beliefs are reinforced and passed on to Iraqi American children. The extended family is the most important social unit to Iraqi Americans. Family comes first–before the individual family member, even before one's job. A family's reputation is very important. It determines a person's status in society. Individuals try to behave in a way that will not shame their family.

In traditional Iraqi American families, the father is the head of the household. Children are expected to obey family elders. As a matter of custom, Iraqi children live with their parents longer than children in America tend to do. Family conflicts do arise, however, when younger family members adopt values of individualism and independence that are part of American society.

Upper-class first-generation Iraqi American women are typically well educated, and many work outside the home. Western-style dress is common. Some women may cover their hair in public. When older women first arrive in America, they may wear an *abaya,* a long cloak that reaches from neck to ankle, but most adopt Western clothing fairly quickly.

Marriage is expected of all young adults. The practice of arranged marriages has continued among Iraqi immigrants, though in some families the arrangements depend upon the approval of the couple involved. Other young people, especially second- and third-generation Iraqi Americans, choose their own mates. Some even marry non-Iraqis. Traditionally, Arab women do not take their husbands' names after marriage. Instead, a woman uses her name and her father's name. For instance, the name Nawal Ali Nasser identifies Nawal as the daughter of Ali of the Nasser family.

Work

Iraqi immigrants who arrived in the United States between 1940 and 1968 were generally well educated and experienced professionals. Since 1980, Iraqi immigrants coming to America are likely to be poor and working-class. A growing number are refugees.

Established Arab communities and groups in the Midwest provide a cushion for many struggling immigrants. Many Arab-owned factories, like textile and paper mills, and businesses, such as construction and insurance companies, help new Arab immigrants get established.

Many Iraqi Americans are part of large family *networks* that have helped them start small businesses. Others are in professions such as medicine, insurance, law, and health care.

Let's Talk

Cultural differences in the way that people talk to one another and make friends can confuse and startle Americans and Iraqis.

In Iraqi culture, body language is as important as spoken language. Iraqis tend to touch each other more when speaking than people of Western cultures do. They also stand closer together than most Americans are used to, making many uncomfortable.

It is not uncommon for Iraqis of the same sex to hold hands while talking. It is a sign of openness. A kiss on the cheek or an embrace is a common greeting between members of the same sex. Members of the opposite sex have no physical contact and never develop friendships with each another. As a result, in America any friendly gesture by a woman may be interpreted as a romantic gesture by Iraqi men.

Many different hand and eye gestures are common among Iraqi men. It is not uncommon for them to be loud and interrupt each other in lively conversations. This is not considered bad manners. They also feel free to ask personal questions about employment, finances, marriage, and children. Iraqi Kurds are used to expressing their opinions bluntly. They don't understand why Americans think this is rude.

School

Iraqi families expect their children to excel in school. Children are disciplined and told not to question authority. Because of the British involvement in Iraq between the early 1900s and 1932, the use of English in Iraq is fairly common. As a result, Iraqi children from urban areas tend to do well in American schools. Most Iraqi students continue on to college or other technical training.

An Iraqi immigrant girl works at spelling at the Stout Middle School in Dearborn, Michigan. Although she attends an American school, she still follows the traditional Muslim dress code that requires women to cover their bodies from head to toe when in public.

Although most Iraqi Kurds value education, their location in remote, mountainous areas makes it difficult for Kurdish children to complete more than a few years of school. Where schools do exist, lessons are in Arabic. Kurdish children are therefore less likely to be exposed to English, especially the written language, and Western culture than Iraqis living in urban areas. For these reasons, Kurdish children experience more problems adjusting to American schools.

Religion

About 95 percent of Iraqi Americans are Muslim, but beliefs vary depending upon which form of Islam each individual follows. About 61 percent are Shi'ite Muslims; the remaining Muslims are Sunni. About 5 percent of the Iraqi population is either Christian or Jewish. Most of the Christians are Armenian and Assyrian Catholics.

Iraqi American Muslim families go to weekly prayer service. The men and boys have access to the altar, while women meet and pray in a separate section away from the altar. For Iraqi Americans, the mosque provides a strong community that reinforces their connections to Iraqi culture and traditions. Many first-generation Iraqi Americans find comfort in the society that surrounds the mosque. Community outreach groups are centered in the mosque, and many social activities, like book discussion groups, sewing and weaving circles, and cooking clubs, keep Iraqi American families bonded.

Iraqi Kurds are predominantly Sunni Muslim, although some are Shi'ite Muslims, as well as Christians. One tribe of Kurds, the Yazidis, believes in a mixture of Christianity, Islam, and Zoroastrianism (an ancient Iranian religion).

Holidays and Festivals

Festivals are happy occasions when Iraqi Americans gather with their families and friends for feasts and socializing. Most Iraqi American celebrations are Islamic religious holidays. The dates for the holidays are based on the Islamic lunar calendar, which means they are celebrated on different days each year.

Shi'ite Muslims observe Ashura during the first ten days of the Islamic New Year. During this time, they remember the death of Hussein, grandson of the Prophet Mohammad.

All Muslims, both Sunni and Shi'ite, observe the holy month of Ramadan. During this time, Muslims do not eat or drink during the day. They reflect upon their relationship with Allah and ask for forgiveness for their sins. The holiday ends with a feast and celebration called Eid al-Fitr. Many people, especially children, get new clothes for the occasion. Friends and family may exchange gifts.

Eid al-Adha, the Feast of the Sacrifice, honors Abraham and his devotion to God. Food for the feast is shared between family members and the poor of the community.

Tree at the Boundary

The story of Tree at the Boundary is told during the Islamic New Year celebration called Muharram. According to legend, on the first night of the new year, an angel shakes a tree at the place, or boundary, where heaven and earth meet. Each leaf on the tree represents a person. If a person's leaf falls off the tree when the angel shakes it, that person will die in the coming year.

The Arts

Thousands of years of civilization have contributed to the great literature, beautiful carpets, and wonderful buildings produced by Iraqis. Under Saddam Hussein's rule, however, the arts have been severely restricted. Portraits of Hussein are one of the only officially approved forms of art.

Iraqi artists who have immigrated to the United States enjoy their newfound freedom. Television, movies, painting, and sculpture are the main arts of modern Iraqi Americans.

Iraqi folk music is played at cultural festivals and religious celebrations. The main instruments used are lutes, drums, and fiddles. Everyone joins in, singing and clapping. A celebration of Arab and Iraqi culture is held once a year in Dearborn, Michigan.

Tile work and carpet weaving are two ancient crafts that modern Iraqis still excel at. Pottery and jewelry making are also popular crafts. Many Iraqi American women enjoy creating these arts.

Food

Hospitality is a long-standing tradition in Iraq. Immigrants have brought this custom with them to America, but cultural differences sometimes cause misunderstandings. Iraqis tend to extend a general invitation to visit. Americans, used to specifying a time and place to get together, often don't consider this a "real" invitation. As a result, many first-generation Iraqis feel that Americans are unfriendly.

Misunderstandings can also occur when Americans offer Iraqi guests food. In most Middle Eastern countries, including Iraq, it is considered polite to refuse food the first few times it's offered. The host offers it again and again, insisting that the guest try it. If Americans are unaware of this custom, they may feel hurt when their guests don't want to eat something they've prepared. And the guests may be hungry the entire visit, wondering why the host doesn't offer the food again.

Iraqi food has much in common with the food of Iran, Turkey, and Greece. Lamb is the

Coffee and Conversation

Making coffee in the traditional Iraqi way takes time. After grinding the coffee beans and brewing the coffee, cool and bring the coffee to a boil nine times to cleanse it. Add fresh cream or milk and sweeten the strong coffee with sugar. Now you're ready for a favorite Iraqi pastime—coffee and conversation with friends.

most common meat, although beef, chicken, and fish are also served. Tea and coffee are usually served before and after meals. Alcohol is forbidden by Islam, as is pork.

Cheese, bread, eggs, and potatoes make up a typical breakfast. A lunch for children might include vegetables, eggs, and cooked chicken rolled up in a pancake. Influenced by Arab American culture, many American fast-food restaurants now serve a similar pita bread roll-up.

An evening meal might include vegetables, potatoes, salad, lemons, bread, and kabobs. Kabobs consist of meat and vegetables placed on a long stick called a skewer. The kabobs are cooked over a grill or in an oven. Boiled lamb with rice is another popular dinner dish, as is *kubba*. In this dish, shells made of wheat and chopped meat are filled with more meat, onions, spices, and nuts. They are then fried and served with vegetables or yogurt.

An Iraqi family in Baghdad gathers for a meal after sundown on the thirteenth day of Ramadan. During the month of Ramadan, devout Muslims refrain from eating and drinking during daylight hours as an act of sacrifice and purification.

Many second- and third-generation Iraqi Americans eat a typical American menu. They may eat traditional Iraqi foods only on special occasions or if cooked by an elder.

Recipe

Date Halvah

8 ounces pitted dates, finely chopped

2 ounces walnuts, finely chopped

2 ounces almonds, finely chopped

1/4 teaspoon ground cinnamon

1/4 teaspoon ground allspice

Powdered sugar

Mix the dates, nuts, and spices in a bowl, using your hands to work the ingredients together. Dust a work surface with powdered sugar. Then roll out the halvah about 3/4 inch thick. (Alternately, place the date and nut mixture on a piece of wax paper. Place another sheet of wax paper over the top of the mixture. Press into a rectangle about 3/4 inch thick.) Cut into 1-inch squares and sprinkle with powdered sugar. Makes 20 to 24 sweets.

Source: Adapted from Food Down Under
http://fooddownunder.com/cgi-bin/recipe.cgi?r=66311

CHAPTER FOUR

Jamaicans

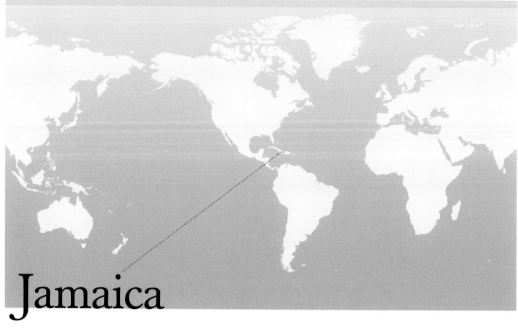

Jamaica

is just 90 miles (144 kilometers) south of Cuba, less than 200 miles (320 kilometers) from the United States. Just a little smaller than the state of Connecticut, Jamaica is the third largest island in the Caribbean but the largest English-speaking island. Most people who come from the English-speaking countries of the region call themselves West Indian or Caribbean.

Until the end of the fifteenth century when Christopher Columbus stumbled upon the islands of the Caribbean, Europeans were not aware that the region existed. The native Arawak (AIR-uh-*wahk*) people called the island Xaymaca–"land of woods and water."

Today, Jamaica is home to people whose *ancestors* have come from all over the world. The island's religions, art, music, language, and food are a mix of its African, Arab, Asian, and European *cultures*. Its motto–"Out of Many, One People"–reflects its commitment to diversity.

Jamaica's Ethnic Groups

a	African	76%
b	Mulatto/ Creole	15%
c	East Indian/ African Indian	3.4%
d	White	3.2%
e	Chinese/ African Chinese	1.2%
f	Other	1.2%

Source: CIA World Factbook, *2002*

A Quick Look Back

The Spanish were the first Europeans to invade and conquer Jamaica. The tobacco grown by the Arawaks, the native people, became popular in Spain, and the settlers quickly established tobacco plantations. The native people were forced to work on the plantations. Within eighty years, nearly all the Arawaks were dead from overwork and the diseases introduced by the Spanish. African slaves soon replaced the Arawaks on the plantations.

In 1655, Jamaica was captured by the British. Before escaping, the Spanish freed their African slaves. These slaves became known as the Maroons. The name probably came from the Spanish word *cimarrón* (see-ma-RON), which means "wild and untamed." About 1,500 Maroons slipped away to hide in the mountains.

Under British rule, plantations grew tobacco and, later, sugarcane. The British brought in new slaves, mainly from West Africa, to work on the plantations. At the end of the seventeenth century, a large group of slaves escaped and joined the Maroons in the mountains. One former slave, named Cudjoe, became leader of these runaway slaves and the Maroons. He began a war with the British that is known as the First Maroon War. Cudjoe and his brothers, Accompong and Johnny, were very brave fighters. The British began to fear their attacks. A peace agreement was signed in 1739, and safety was guaranteed to the Maroons and the runaway slaves. Most present-day Maroons continue to live in Moore Town, Accompong Town, and Maroon Town. They police themselves and maintain a special identity in Jamaica.

Did you know?

In 1492, Christopher Columbus set out from Spain to find a new trade route to the East Indies, the area now known as India and Southeast Asia. When land was sighted, Columbus declared that he had discovered the westernmost islands of the Indies and named the area the West Indies. This name is still used to describe the group of islands in the Caribbean Sea.

Did you know?

The Arawaks migrated from South America to Jamaica around 700 B.C. Between 60,000 and 100,000 Arawaks were living in Jamaica when the Spanish landed. Arawak cave paintings and tools that have been found around the island show that the native people were very skilled. One of their inventions, a hanging bed of cotton tied by ropes at each end, impressed the Spanish so much that they brought this Arawak bed design, called a hammock, back to Europe. Hammocks are still used by people today.

Slavery

During the 1600s and 1700s, millions of Africans were sold into slavery and shipped to the West Indies to work. They were crammed onto slave ships and chained together. The trip from West Africa to the West Indies took two to three months. It is thought that one-third of the slaves died on the voyage.

End of Slavery

When slavery in Britain ended in 1838, the British brought *indentured laborers* from China and India to work on the plantations. These newcomers agreed to work for low wages for a set period of time. In return, the plantation owners paid for the voyage from Asia to Jamaica. Many of these workers remained in Jamaica after their period of indenture ended.

For the next 100 years, there were conflicts between workers and plantation owners. Sales of sugarcane were decreasing, but exports of logwood, coffee, and bananas grew. The *economy* began to move away from its dependence on the plantation and the sugarcane crop.

The Rebellion of 1938

As the twentieth century began, African Jamaicans were still being manipulated by the plantation system which directed who got the best land and jobs. People of lighter skin color received better jobs and more respect, while most African Jamaicans were very poor and had no political power.

America's Great Depression in the 1930s hit Jamaica hard. Many Jamaicans who had moved to other countries to work during the 1920s and 1930s returned to the island, only to find few jobs available. The price of sugar and sugarcane fell to an all-time low. Thousands of sugarcane workers and dockworkers had their salaries slashed or lost their jobs.

In the mid-1930s, fed up with poor living conditions, low wages, and high prices, workers began to strike. The protests spread throughout Jamaica and peaked in 1938 with violent riots. Although the rebellion had started as a labor protest, it developed into a political tidal wave with growing demands for independence from Britain.

Marcus Garvey, Norman Manley, and William Alexander Bustamante were instrumental in organizing the protests calling for independence from Britain.

Marcus Mosiah Garvey

Marcus Mosiah Garvey was a leader in the black nationalist ("Back to Africa") movement. Born in Jamaica in 1887, he founded the Universal Negro Improvement Association (UNIA) in 1914. The organization's goal was to create a new country in Africa governed by blacks. UNIA was not very successful in Jamaica, but it grew rapidly when a branch was established in the United States. At its peak, the organization had over 4 million members. Garvey traveled in the United States and all over the world preaching his message of black pride. He inspired American black leaders like Malcolm X to continue the fight for equal rights.

Independent Rule

From 1944 to 1962, Jamaica's economy moved from dependence upon one crop (sugarcane) to an economy centered on farming, bauxite (*box*-ite) and alumina mining (bauxite and alumina are used in the production of aluminum and other products), and the tourist industry. Jamaica's natural beauty and mild climate began to draw tourists from all over the world. Many Jamaicans began to work in hotels, restaurants, and shops related to the tourist industry. The United States became Jamaica's main trading partner, replacing Britain in that role.

Jamaica became an independent country within the British Commonwealth in 1962. A governor-general representing the British Crown, the *Parliament* (*par*-luh-munt), and a high court make up the government. Jamaican voters elect members of the House of Representatives, but the twenty-one members of the Senate are appointed by the governor-general. The appointments are based on recommendations by the leaders of the political parties. The Jamaica Labor Party (JLP), founded by Alexander Bustamante, was elected as the ruling party for the first two terms after independence.

Through most of the 1970s, the People's National Party (PNP) was the ruling party. The PNP started several programs designed to protect and help the poorest in Jamaica, including health care, housing, and education programs. Unfortunately, the country did not have the money to finance these programs. As a result, Jamaica's government went deeply into debt.

The PNP also sought to establish relationships with other *Third World,* or developing, nations. The PNP wanted a relationship with Cuba, an island country just north of Jamaica that shares many ethnic similarities, and the former Soviet Union, instead of the United States. In the mid-1970s the PNP began to move away from a *capitalist,* or free market, economy to *socialism*. Many wanted to try a socialist system in order to divide the island's wealth more equally between the rich and the poor. This shift to socialism cooled relations between Jamaica and the United States. At the same time, a depressed mining industry combined with high oil and food prices, a large government debt, and a downturn in the world economy to make life difficult for many Jamaicans. There were few jobs to be found. People were upset and angry, and in the late 1970s, riots and violence broke out across Jamaica. Rival political gangs fought in the streets. Tourists avoided Jamaica because of the violence.

Finally, the government asked for aid from the International Monetary Fund, the World Bank, and the United Nations. The economic policies of the Jamaican government have been guided by these groups since that time.

The JLP returned to office in the 1980s. The new government worked to repair the relationship with the United States. As a result, Jamaica received aid and money from the U.S. government in the early 1980s. A stronger business link was also forged. Slowly, the mining industry recovered. Tourists flowed into Jamaica from the United States. Even with these changes, Jamaica was still in debt. Making payments on the debt meant that little money was available for programs to help the Jamaican people. A steady *migration* to America ensued.

Jamaica Today

Since 1992, the prime minister of Jamaica has been Percival James Patterson of the PNP. Modern Jamaica faces high rates on borrowed money, growing foreign competition, and continuing debt payments.

Most people still live in small villages in the countryside and work on the land. But pressures on these small-town groups are rising. Twenty percent of the people are unemployed. No jobs in the country towns means that people have to leave their homes to find work. Poverty and anger over the economy have again led to violence. There have been riots, and the crime rate is increasing.

In the mid-1990s, the United States, Germany, and Japan canceled or reduced Jamaica's debt to them. Although the Jamaican and other governments are trying to help, many Jamaicans still look to the United States for a brighter future.

Speaking Jamaican

Although the official language of Jamaica is English, the everyday language of Jamaica is patois (PAT-wah). This musical speech is a mix of English, Spanish, Portuguese, African phrases, and Jamaican slang. Jamaicans try to keep their special language alive by speaking it at home.

New York Massachusetts
Connecticut
New Jersey
Maryland
Florida

Coming to America

J amaicans have come to the United States in a series of migrations since the early 1900s. These migrations have been tied to the need for workers in the United States and changes in U.S. laws. The migrations also reflect political and economic troubles in Jamaica.

Jamaican Population in the U.S.	
New York	257,671
Florida	162,658
Connecticut	27,256
New Jersey	26,946
Maryland	21,039
Massachusetts	20,125

Source: U.S. Census, 2000

U.S./Jamaican Immigration by Decade

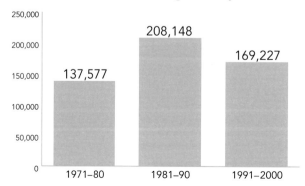

1971–80	1981–90	1991–2000
137,577	208,148	169,227

Source: Statistical Yearbook of the Immigration and Naturalization Service

Today, Jamaicans make their homes in communities across America. The majority lives in the New York City area. Miami, Florida, is home to the second largest Jamaican American community in the United States.

Life in America

J amaican immigrants in America have an advantage over many other immigrant groups: they speak English. Many still go through a period of adjustment, however, when their expectations don't fit the reality of life in America. For some, the dream of life in a middle-class neighborhood is replaced with the reality of life in a poor neighborhood. The expectation that Americans will be as tolerant of racial diversity as Jamaicans is often crushed by the reality of prejudice. Many Jamaicans face prejudice and racism for the first time in America. Although much of the prejudice comes from nonblack Americans, Jamaicans also face prejudice from African Americans, who say that Jamaicans sound too white. A different stereotype works in their favor, however: their British-tinged accents lead some employers to view Jamaicans as highly educated and motivated, giving them an edge in the workplace. This experience has motivated some Jamaican American youth to retain or develop a Jamaican accent.

Family

The extended family is very important to Jamaicans, especially as immigrants in America. They often "adopt" trusted American friends and consider them part of their family. This openness to new people and this skill in making friends ensure the success of Jamaicans.

Many Jamaican and Jamaican American families are matriarchal. This means that the mother, rather than the father or both parents together, is the head of the family. The woman plays a strong role and makes decisions for the family. This seems to be, at least in part, a holdover from slavery days when slaves were not allowed to get married. Today, this family structure is supported by economic factors that force many Jamaican men to leave their families to find work. Women are left behind to hold the extended family together.

Historically, immigration laws discouraged single women from coming to America. Immigration officials assumed that they would need public assistance, especially if they had

Jamericans

Some second-generation Jamaican-American youths call themselves "Jamericans" to show how their two cultures have combined.

children. After 1965, many Jamaican women *immigrated* through the family preferences program. As industrial jobs decreased, the number of Jamaican men entering America slowed down. At the same time, more Jamaican women took advantage of a demand for nurses and domestic help to immigrate to America.

Many Jamaican American families continue the Jamaican tradition of susu, a "saving circle" that can have ten to fifty members. Members contribute a set amount of money each week. They then take turns receiving all the money collected that week. The money is used for emergencies, to help with living costs, or as a fund to send back to friends and family in need in Jamaica.

Keeping island traditions alive encourages Jamaicans, too. These traditions, like celebrating festivals in America, speaking patois, listening to Jamaican music, and teaching their children Jamaican games and stories, make the family stronger. Reading Anansi stories, fables about a crafty spiderman, is one way Jamaican parents pass along their culture to their children. Slaves brought these stories from the west coast of Africa to Jamaica more than 200 years ago.

Work

As writers, engineers, doctors, lawyers, filmmakers, artists, actors, and businesspeople, Jamaicans have made the United States a better, more interesting place. Many early immigrants worked hard in factories or as domestics in order to save money and get college degrees. The English skills of later Jamaican immigrants gave them entry into high-level jobs, especially in the 1970s and 1980s. Many Jamaicans became professionals who were able to provide money and support to the next generation of immigrants. A nursing and health care worker shortage in the United States in the 1980s and 1990s also attracted many Jamaicans, particularly women immigrants. Although many Jamaicans hold high-level positions in the United States, some feel that a "glass ceiling" keeps them from reaching the top of their professions.

Jamaican entrepreneurs have transformed many American neighborhoods, opening small businesses to serve their community. Many of these small operations have grown into large companies. Jamaican Americans have found success in publishing, taxi companies, real estate, advertising, banking, insurance, and retail clothing.

Spotlight on
PATRICK EWING

Patrick Ewing of National Basketball Association (NBA) fame was born in Kingston, Jamaica, on January 5, 1962, the day before Jamaica's independence was declared. He played cricket and soccer as a youngster in Jamaica before moving in 1975 to Cambridge, Massachusetts, where he first played basketball. Ewing graduated from Georgetown University with a degree in fine arts. He considers that his best achievement.

After graduation, Ewing was drafted by the New York Knicks. His salary, $1.7 million, was the highest ever paid to a rookie. He has had an all-star career in the NBA, first with the Knicks and more recently for the Orlando Magic. One of the highlights of Ewing's career came in 1992 when he was a member of America's basketball "Dream Team," winning the gold medal at the summer Olympics in Barcelona, Spain.

Patrick Ewing, who was born in Jamaica, jumps for his 10,000th rebound in a game against the Phoenix Suns. Ewing is one of only twelve National Basketball Association players to score at least 20,000 points and grab 10,000 rebounds. His number 33 has been retired by the New York Knicks in honor of his many accomplishments on the court.

School

Jamaicans believe in the value of a good education. In fact, many early immigrants came to America to further their education. This respect for education has aided many second-generation Jamaican Americans. It has also contributed to their representation in America's black middle and upper class.

This tradition can cause conflicts in families when Jamaican parents view American students as lazy or disrespectful and discourage their children from spending time with their friends. The extra opportunities that American schools offer, including computers and a full library, are welcome, however.

School, Island-Style

Jamaicans view education as the best way for children to do well and succeed in life. Education is so important to Jamaicans that strangers often stop children on the street and ask why they are not in school. As a result, Jamaica has a high literacy rate: 92 percent of the population can read.

The Jamaican school day begins at 8:00 A.M. and ends at 1:30 P.M. because the hot afternoons make it uncomfortable to remain in the classroom. Some schools offer extra lessons for students who are interested. There may be up to sixty pupils in a classroom. Students wear school uniforms, usually in the school colors.

The children at Jamaican schools have several vacations. They have one week off at Easter, three months in the summer, three days for National Heroes Week, two days for Labor Day, and two weeks during the Christmas and New Year's holiday period.

All Jamaican children participate in some type of sports at school. Soccer, swimming, cricket, field hockey, tennis, netball, and basketball are popular choices.

Spotlight on
COLIN POWELL

Secretary of State Colin Powell answers questions from reporters about U.S. policy issues. Powell's parents emigrated from Jamaica before he was born. The secretary of state is responsible for U.S. foreign policy and is fourth in the order of presidential succession.

Secretary of State Colin Powell is Jamaican American. His parents, Luther and Maud Powell, immigrated to the United States from Jamaica during the Great Depression. Colin Powell was born in New York City on April 5, 1937, and was raised in the South Bronx. He was educated in the New York City public schools, graduating from the City College of New York, where he earned a bachelor's degree in geology. Powell received his commission as a U.S. Army second lieutenant upon his graduation in 1958. He later earned a master's degree in business administration from George Washington University in Washington, D.C.

Powell was a professional soldier for thirty-five years, rising to the rank of a four-star general. During the 1991 Gulf War, he served as chairman of the Joint Chiefs of Staff. In this position, he advised the president about military strategy that led to a victory over Iraq.

Following his retirement from the army, he wrote his best-selling autobiography, *My American Journey*. Over his lifetime, Powell has received two Presidential Medals of Freedom, the President's Citizen's Medal, the Congressional Gold Medal, and the Secretary of State Distinguished Service Medal. One of Powell's proudest associations has been with America's Promise, an alliance for youth. This organization is dedicated to building support from every part of society to fund education and develop the character and competence of young people.

When George W. Bush became president in 2000, he chose Colin Powell as secretary of state. In this position, Powell serves as America's top diplomat.

Religion

Religion is a very important part of life for West Indians. Most Jamaicans and Jamaican Americans, about 75 percent, are Christians. French and Spanish colonists introduced Roman Catholicism to the Caribbean. Protestant Christian churches, including Anglican, Baptist, and Methodist, were established in Jamaica by the British and Americans. During the first decades of the twentieth century, Jamaican American churches in New York's Harlem and Brooklyn neighborhoods became the focus of life for newly arrived Jamaican Americans. In Presbyterian, Catholic, Episcopal, and African Methodist Episcopal churches, Jamaican-born ministers moved into leadership roles. Pastors of Caribbean immigrant parishes became politically active in the 1920s and 1930s.

Churches took on an importance beyond worship alone: They became a piece of home or a link with home. Within the church, island culture could be preserved. Caribbean-style celebrations of harvests, Christmas, New Year's, and Jamaican Emancipation Day were held in the church. Weddings and funerals were celebrated on a large scale, island-style. Second- and third-generation Jamaicans, however, have moved away from elaborate and expensive island funerals and weddings.

Caribbean churches give a safe social space to young Jamaican Americans. Youth activities and counseling within the churches provide guidance and encouragement. Many young Jamaican Americans whose parents both work or who have only one parent have found an extended family in the church.

Descendants of Asians who came to Jamaica as indentured workers in the nineteenth century have kept their religions—Islam, Judaism, and Hinduism—alive as well. However, Jamaican Americans of East Indian descent are concerned that their Hindu religion and traditions will be lost. In New York and other cities with a large Jamaican Hindu community, the influence of American dress, television, music, movies, streets, and schools is seen to be pulling children away from a rich Hindu culture.

A religion called Rastafarianism (rah-stuh-*far*-ee-un-izm) has become very popular among Jamaican people of African descent. It is based on the Bible, the speeches of Haile Selassie I, the last Ethiopian emperor, and Marcus Garvey, the leader of the black nationalist movement in the 1920s. Rastafarians, or Rastas, wear their hair in long braids called dreadlocks. Like Muslims and Jews, Rastas do not eat pork. Many are vegetarians. Reggae music is very important to Rastafarianism. Tens of thousands of Rastafarians live in New York City, making up the largest group of Rastas outside of Jamaica. Rastas have established many churches, political associations, and community and day care centers. The Rasta religion in the United States is changing. More women are gaining an active role in the church, working to end *discrimination* and domestic violence and to encourage education. Traditional Rastafarianism in Jamaica is led only by men.

Did you know?

Rastafarian men usually wear a brightly colored woolen knitted hat, called a tam, at an angle on their long, braided hair. They wash their hair with soap that is allowed to dry in the hair. Then, they tie their hair into knots or braids. These braids, called dreadlocks, are inspired by the hair of Masai and Ethiopian tribes in east Africa.

The dreadlocks are a sign of faith for Rastafarian men. They let their hair grow because they believe that the Bible forbids them to cut their hair.

Folk religions like Santeria have gained followers in America. Santeria has its roots in West African culture. It supports the use of magic and potions for solving problems. Santeria beliefs may be held along with Christian beliefs, as when people use Voodoo candles or potions in a Catholic church.

Holidays and Festivals

Jamaican American festivals generally feature a lively mixture of music and food. Immigrants have brought their religious celebrations, including Christmas, Eid al-Fitr, and Diwali, with them to America as well.

Jamaican Christmas traditions are very similar to those in America. Santa Claus brings gifts to well-behaved children on Christmas Eve. Family and friends gather for religious services and feasts, including the Christmas fruitcake. Jamaican Americans also enjoy many of the same Christmas carols, although they are usually set to reggae (REG-ay), a Jamaican musical style.

In America, Jamaican Muslims celebrate Eid al-Fitr, the feast at the end of the holy month of Ramadan, in the same manner as other Muslims. Feasting, gift exchanges, and socializing are all part of the celebration.

Diwali is the Hindu festival of light, held in mid-November. The Hindu community in New York decorates homes and businesses with big lighted displays as well as the traditional lamps. In many cases, the lights are left up through the Christmas season. Friends and family members exchange gifts and greetings. They take up donations of food, money, and clothing for those in need and have a feast with family and friends.

Jamaicans and other immigrants from the Caribbean region have introduced Carnival celebrations to the United States. Carnival was originally a Roman Catholic festival held just before Lent, the forty-day period leading up to Easter. For

Rastafarian

The name "Rastafarian" comes from the given name of Ethiopian emperor Haile Selassie I. Before he became emperor and took a royal name, he was known as Ras Tafari. Rastafarians believe that Selassie fulfilled a prophecy by black leader Marcus Garvey in the 1920s. Garvey's writings and philosophy are part of the foundation of Rasta beliefs.

Master drummer Cedric "Im" Brooks, a well-known reggae musician, was born in Jamaica and is a Rastafarian.

Jamaicans, Carnival in America has become a big party that celebrates their Caribbean heritage and their new home. It is a time to dance and sing and have fun. People parade through the streets in brightly colored costumes and masks and dance to the music of steel drum bands or reggae. Today, Carnival celebrations are held throughout America, but there is one important difference between American and Caribbean Carnivals. In America, Carnival is usually celebrated in the summer months to take advantage of warmer weather. In the Caribbean, the celebrations are still held before Easter, usually in March or April.

The Arts

In the 1920s, a movement called the Harlem Renaissance marked a new era in American art, music, and literature. Named for the Harlem neighborhood in New York City where it flowered, the movement had its roots in African Americans' newfound feelings of freedom and black identity. West Indians in America found a way to express themselves in this movement, too. In fact, one of the most important writers in the Harlem Renaissance, Claude McKay, was born in Jamaica. In his many essays and plays, he represented black people as self-confident and free.

Children dress in native costumes and dance in the annual Kiddie Caribbean Parade in Brooklyn, New York, to celebrate the traditions and culture of the peoples of the Caribbean.

Reggae music is perhaps the most well-known musical import from Jamaica to the United States. Jamaican Bob Marley helped to make this style of music popular all over the world. Reggae began in the early 1970s, but its roots go back farther than that. It is a mix of rhythm and blues and early Jamaican music. Reggae songs are about life on the Jamaican streets. Because of Rastafarian influence, the songs also talk about peace, love, and forgiveness. Electric guitar and organ are a part of reggae's special beat and sound. It has been called the "heartbeat of the island."

Spotlight on
BOB MARLEY

Jamaican singer and song-writer Bob Marley is shown during a performance. Marley's blend of Rastafarianism and reggae music was embraced by people throughout the world. Hundreds of thousands of his fans, including the prime minister of Jamaica, attended his funeral. His music is still popular today.

Born in Nine Mile, Jamaica, in 1945, Bob Marley was twelve years old when he moved with his mother to the capital city of Kingston. At fifteen, he formed his first band. Two years later, he recorded his first album, *Judge Not,* with his band, the Wailing Wailers. The band became known as the Wailers and traveled in the United States and Britain. Musical stars like Eric Clapton and Barbra Streisand recorded some of Marley's songs and made Marley famous.

In the 1970s, Marley's music became important in religious and political movements in Jamaica. The special sound of reggae and its street roots were heard around the world. Even though Marley became rich and famous, he never forgot that he came from a ghetto. His songs celebrate the poor and their strength. Today the Bob Marley Caribbean Festival, held each year in Miami, Florida, raises thousands of dollars for humanitarian projects.

Bob Marley died in 1981. He was laid to rest in the village of his childhood, Nine Mile, Jamaica.

Food

Jamaican food reflects the people who came to the island from West Africa, Europe, India, and China as well as the native Caribs. As Jamaican immigrants settle in the United States and Americans travel to Jamaica for vacations, the flavors of Jamaican and Caribbean cooking are becoming more common in America.

One of Jamaica's spiciest foods, jerk, can be traced to the native Arawak people. In order to preserve meat and fish, the Arawaks coated the food with a pepper sauce, then grilled it. This early form of barbecue was also used by the Maroons, slaves freed by the Spanish, who later fled to the mountains to avoid British enslavement.

Many foods, such as bananas, mangoes, coconuts, oranges, avocados, and limes were introduced to the island by European settlers and traders. African slaves brought yams with them to the West Indies. Indentured laborers from Asia brought spices and curries.

The national dish of Jamaica, akee and salt fish, combines English and African foods. Salted fish was a popular English dish. Akee fruit was originally brought from West Africa. The soft yellow akees taste like scrambled eggs when they are cooked. This spicy dish is usually served with breadfruit or fried dumplings. In America, canned akee is much easier to find than the fresh fruits, although markets in New York and Miami often carry them. Another favorite food that was influenced by the British is patties, or pasties. These are small, flat pies filled with spicy chicken, salt fish, or beef.

Recipe

Coconut Milkshake

2 cups vanilla ice cream

2 cups coconut milk, chilled

1 cup milk, chilled

Pinch of freshly grated nutmeg

Ice cubes

Combine all the ingredients except the ice cubes in a blender and liquefy. Place the ice cubes in tall, chilled glasses. Fill the glasses with the milkshake. Serve immediately.

Serves 2 to 4.

Source: Dorinda's Taste of the Caribbean *by Dorinda Hafner*

CHAPTER FIVE

Kenyans

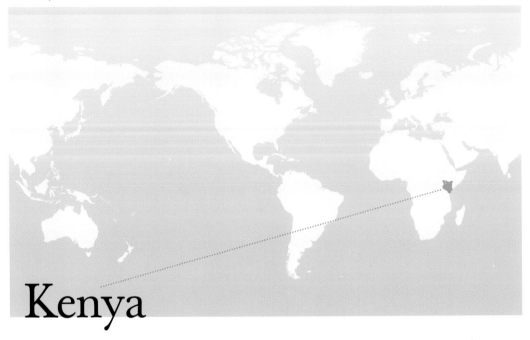

Kenya

The people and cultures of Kenya are as diverse as the spectacular wildlife for which the country is best known. Almost all of Kenya's 28 million people are native Africans, representing over forty ethnic groups and many different languages. The rest are of Arab, Asian, and European descent. The largest of the native groups is the Kikuyu (key-KOO-yu), who live in the central region along with the Kamba. The Kikuyu, Kamba, and Luhya people, who live in western Kenya, all speak a form of Bantu, as do the people of many smaller tribes. The Luo (LOO-oh) people farm and fish on the shores of Lake Victoria in western Kenya. Their language has much in common with those of the Kalenjin in southern Kenya and the Masai (ma-SIGH), a nomadic tribe that lives in the eastern plains.

Members of a Masai family with their cattle travel through a dry river basin as they move in search of water near Nairobi, Kenya.

The number of tribal languages often makes communication difficult between groups. As a result, Kenya has two official languages: *Kiswahili* (*kee*-swa-HE-lee), a Bantu language that is widely used in eastern Africa, and English, the language introduced by British colonists. (Kiswahili is also known as Swahili.) English is used in most business dealings, schools, and the government.

Although Kenya is considered one of the most successful countries in Africa, tribal tensions, *drought* (drout), and overcrowding are causing many Kenyans to seek new opportunities and a more secure life in the United States.

A Quick Look Back

Kenya has existed as a nation only in modern times. Its borders were drawn by European settlers at the end of the nineteenth century. While early Africans left no written history, some archeologists who have studied bone pieces and tools from the Great Rift Valley that runs through western Kenya believe that human ancestors were living there more than 1 million years ago. Many people think the valley is where human life first developed.

The ancestors of modern-day Kenyans began arriving in east Africa about 2,000 years ago. Bantu-speaking tribes, including the Kikuyu, arrived first. Primarily farmers, these people also knew how to make iron. Soon the Nilotic (ni-LOT-ik) and Cushitic (koo-SHI-tik) tribes began to move into the region from the north. The Nilotic people include the Masai and the Samburu tribes, while the Somalis are Cushitic. (The ethnic Somali who live in Kenya are related to the people of Somalia, Kenya's neighbor to the east.) These tribes are still nomads, or wanderers.

The Arrival of the British

European explorers from Britain, Germany, and France arrived in Kenya in the mid-1800s. Through trade and religious missionaries, Europeans began to gain power in east Africa in the 1880s. The European powers met and carved up Africa, each nation deciding which part of Africa it would take. The British chose Kenya and Uganda, hoping to protect their interests in Egypt and the source of the Nile River near Lake Victoria.

The British built a railway to connect Uganda to Kenya's coast. The line ended in Nairobi and a city grew up around it, which would later become the nation's capital. In 1900, British citizens were invited to settle along the railway. In return, the British government gave them large pieces of land— land that was forcibly taken from Kenya's people. Within fifteen years, there were over 5,000 British farmers in Kenya. Workers from China and India were brought in by the British, too.

People of Kenya

a	Kikuyu	22%
b	Luhya	14%
c	Luo	13%
d	Kalenjin	12%
e	Kamba	11%
f	Kisii	6%
g	Meru	6%
h	Asian, European, Arab	1%
i	Other African	15%

Source: World Factbook *2002*

These developments marked a major change in Kenya's *economy.* Before this time, farming was primarily a means of feeding one's family. The British introduced large-scale agricultural production of crops intended for export, such as coffee, tea, and wheat. Africans were not allowed to grow cash crops such as these, however. In order to pay the taxes that the British demanded, they had to work on the plantations where the crops were grown or move to cities and work in the new manufacturing plants. Money was also introduced in Kenya at this time; earlier, people had bartered or traded for items they needed.

After World War I, many British soldiers came to Kenya. The best land in the highlands was reserved for these and other white settlers. Kenyans who had lived in these areas often had no option but to work on the British plantations. Without their land, they had no other way to earn a living.

European missionaries set up schools in Kenya. As Kenyans became more educated, they began to question Britain's rule. The Kikuyu Central Association formed to protest Britain's actions in Kenya. One of its leaders, Jomo Kenyatta, went to England in 1929 and 1931 to demand the return of African lands and to push for increased economic opportunities, but he had little success. He remained in Europe for fifteen years, forming alliances with other African leaders and promoting independence for Kenya.

Call for Independence

Kenyatta returned to Kenya in 1946. He soon became president of the Kenya African Union (KAU), a two-year-old political party. Although Kenyatta and most of its members were from the Kikuyu tribe, he worked tirelessly to establish unity among all the tribes. The main goal of the political party was for Africans in Kenya to be represented in the government. In 1951, the KAU presented a list of demands to the British government. They were rejected.

When diplomacy failed to work, the Mau Mau *guerrilla* movement began a violent campaign to scare British settlers off the land that had belonged to the Kipsigis, Masai, and Nandi tribes. The guerrillas killed cattle belonging to white settlers as well as the cattle of any Africans who supported them. The Mau Mau later escalated the violence, killing thirty-two white

Mau Mau

The Mau Mau got their name from a Kikuyu word that describes the sound a hyena makes as it eats its prey.

farmers. The British government responded with attacks that killed thousands of Africans. World opinion began to turn against Britain and its role in Africa.

Former Mau Mau guerrillas and their families sing revolutionary songs from the 1950s at a commemoration of the fiftieth anniversary of their movement in Nyeri, Kenya.

Although the KAU didn't support the actions of the Mau Mau, in 1952 the British arrested Jomo Kenyatta and other KAU leaders in response to the violence. Kenyatta had spoken out many times against British rule in Kenya. As leader of a political party that was drawing more and more support from Kenyans, he was considered a threat to the British government. He remained in jail almost nine years.

Independence

The push for independence continued despite Britain's efforts to provide more opportunities for political involvement to Kenya's people. The British began to feel that independence was inevitable. Finally, in 1961, Britain began preparing to withdraw from Kenya. In 1963, Kenya became an independent country. Jomo Kenyatta was elected president. He tried to unite the different tribes and urged whites and blacks to build a stronger Kenya together. Through the 1960s and 1970s, the economy grew as more Africans began to grow crops for export. Coffee, tea, and sugarcane were the main products during this period.

When President Kenyatta died in 1978, his vice president, Daniel arap Moi, became president. During his first few years in office, Moi continued Kenyatta's policies. However, as the economy slowed in the early 1980s, he took greater control of the government. His authoritarian style disturbed many Kenyans, and he faced an attempted *coup* in 1982.

With thousands of Kenyans unemployed, protests against Moi's government increased. Moi began to arrest the protesters and shut down newspapers that voiced opinions against him. The tourism industry, which brought in millions of dollars each year, grew shaky because of the continued political instability.

In 1992, Moi gave in to pressure from the international community and allowed multiparty elections. Moi won the 1992 election as well as the 1997 election because the vote was split among his rivals. The 1990s were marked by increasing corruption in the Kenyan government and a stagnating or declining economy. The Kenyan people were ready for change.

Kenya Today

In December 2002, Mwai Kibaki (m-WHY kee-BAH-kee) was elected president of Kenya by a landslide. He has promised to fight corruption in the government, provide free education to elementary students, and improve health care. He is inheriting serious problems with the economy, since an estimated 50 percent of Kenyans live in poverty.

The economic decline that Kenya has experienced has contributed to increased racial and ethnic tensions.

New difficulties are also growing with neighboring Ethiopia and Somalia. Thousands of *refugees* from these countries flee to safety in Kenya. At first, the Kenyan government tried to turn them away. But the United Nations (UN) asked Kenya to help the refugees. With a drought and an economy that is sliding downward, the Kenyan government is pressed to provide for its own people and has few resources to give to the refugees. The UN and other international agencies are providing medicine and food to Kenyans as well as the refugees.

This volatile combination of political, racial, and economic tensions makes many Kenyans afraid that their country will suffer the same violent uprisings that their neighbors have suffered.

Wildlife versus People

In recent years, Kenya has set aside large areas of land for the protection of wildlife. In addition, hunting has been banned throughout the country in order to save endangered species.

Kenya's government has made an effort to protect its wildlife because it is profitable for the tourist industry. However, the size of the park system in Kenya makes it difficult to police. Gangs of poachers from inside and outside the country raid the parks and kill animals. Kenyan farmers feel that the wild animals take up land that could be used for grazing cattle.

Natural disasters, like the long periods of drought that Kenya has experienced recently, have also caused problems in the parks. The rhinoceros and elephant populations are decreasing. People in these areas compete with the wild animals for the food and water they need to survive.

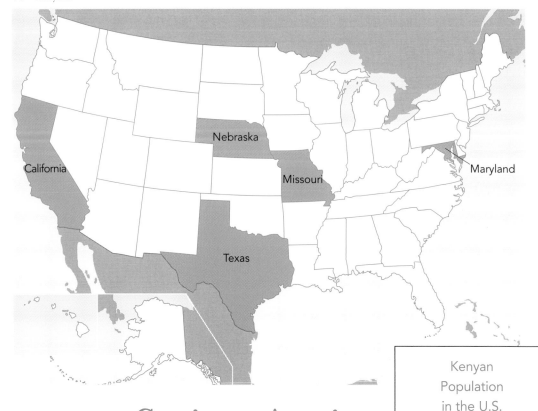

Nebraska

California

Missouri

Maryland

Texas

Coming to America

Kenyans have traveled to the United States for many years. Some came to the United States on business. Others enrolled in American colleges and universities. Until recently, only a few thought about settling in the United States. This was partly because of strict quotas, or limits, on the number of immigrants from African countries before 1965. It was also due to America's history of slavery and racism. One of the biggest reasons that few Kenyans immigrated to America, however, was their hope for the future of their country after achieving independence in 1963.

Most Kenyans who do immigrate to the United States settle in

Kenyan Population in the U.S.	
Maryland	3,811
Missouri	3,364
Texas	2,062
California	1,081
Nebraska	1,079

Source: U.S. Census, 2000

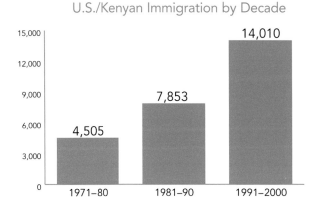

U.S./Kenyan Immigration by Decade

	14,010
7,853	
4,505	
1971–80	1981–90	1991–2000

Source: Statistical Yearbook of the Immigration and Naturalization Service

cities. One of the largest Kenyan communities in America is found in the Washington, D.C. area, especially in the state of Maryland. Other Kenyan immigrants have established communities in Missouri and Texas.

Life in America

Because Kenyans come from a tribal culture, they sometimes find American life isolating. The intense influence of American popular culture, in television and movies, in products and advertisements, seems to put at risk the quieter, more hidden rhythms of Kenyan traditions and culture.

Kenyans arrive in the United States never having experienced a culture where they are not part of the majority. They are not prepared for the *discrimination* they encounter. Some Kenyans face an identity crisis. They are expected to automatically have a common bond with other African Americans, but sometimes they feel they have more in common with other American ethnic groups.

Family

Family is very important to Kenyans. Family connections extend to many people within tribal units. Relationships, no matter how distant, are honored and welcomed. Kenyans in America reach out to family and village or tribal members back in Kenya. Elderly members of families are honored and cared for, even if they remain in Kenya. Kenyans in America often send money home to family and village members.

Within tribes in Kenya, marriages are arranged at a young age. Once in America, Kenyans still look to their immediate community for marriage partners, but arranged marriages are fewer. Kenyan American women tend to wait longer to marry than their Kenyan counterparts. The possibility of higher education and careers delays marriage and the start of a family. Kenyan American men are learning to help with chores and child care, but Kenyan American women still bear most of the responsibility of caring for children. Elder women relatives, aunts and grandmothers, help Kenyan American families with child care, too. Because of their tradition of caring for extended family, some Kenyan Americans find themselves pulled in many directions. At times the noise of busy American life and the stress of juggling work, family, and extended family threaten to overwhelm their families and their customs. Kenyans from rural areas feel a special anxiety. Those from Nairobi and other large cities in Kenya adapt more easily.

In American cities with large Kenyan communities, such as in the Washington, D.C. area, Kenyan and African organizations introduce young people to the traditions and language of their homeland. These programs help students learn or maintain their native language so they can talk with relatives and friends when they visit Kenya. The organizations also give young people a better understanding of their identity. Children are less likely to be affected by negative influences in their school or neighborhood, like gangs and drugs, if they maintain ties to their heritage.

Kigogo

Kigogo, also called *mancala*, is a popular game in Africa. It has made its way around the world, including America. Although it seems simple, the mathematical strategies involved in winning make some versions of the game as complex as chess.

The *kigogo* game board is a rectangular piece of wood with two rows of hollowed-out places or cups. A larger cup, called the *mancala*, is located at each end of the board. Seeds, stones, or shells are moved around the board. The object of the game is to capture as many of the other player's game pieces as possible while moving your own pieces around the board.

Work

Work opportunities for Kenyans in the United States are growing as Kenyan Americans connect and begin to focus on how to help each other. Many come to the United States with a strong educational background. They already know English and do not have problems finding work. Kenyans from remote tribal areas may or may not be educated. Even for those who are educated, their work experience is usually related to agriculture and may not apply to the jobs available in the area where they settle. If they do not speak English, they are likely to be stuck in a low-paying service job. Many immigrants who are not adept at English look for work as taxi drivers, security guards, and restaurant workers upon first arriving in America.

As the Kenyan and African community grows, more immigrants open their own businesses. In 2000, Kenyan Americans sponsored a conference on entrepreneurship at William Paterson University in Wayne, New Jersey. The focus was on networking and building business contacts both here and in Kenya. Kenyan Americans love their homeland and hope to use their work experience here to help revive the Kenyan economy and improve conditions for family and friends back home. The conference also encouraged Kenyan Americans who were enrolled in college to pursue professional careers in America.

Like other African American immigrant groups, Kenyan Americans often join savings clubs. Each member of the club puts a certain amount of money into the club each week or month. When an emergency occurs or a loan is needed to begin a business, the club member may draw out money.

School

Education is an elusive goal for many Kenyans. Until President Kibaki took office at the end of 2002, many Kenyans could not afford to pay the fees for their children's schools. As a result, many families come to America so their children can receive a good education and go on to college. Because most Kenyans speak English, they have an easier time with their studies than other immigrant groups. However, Kenyan students have also had to put up with name-calling and teasing, from both white and African American classmates who consider them too foreign.

Ruth Sakuda (left) gets a hug from her son Moses Sakuda after he graduated from Eastern Mennonite University in Harrisonburg, Virginia, with a master's of divinity degree and a master's of art in education. Moses Sakuda plans to earn a doctorate in business administration before returning to Kenya.

One student was shocked to find out that her dream of America was so wrong. She found that most American students were ignorant about Kenya. Both black and white students called her names and told her to go back where she came from. Black students thought she was acting stuck-up because of her British accent. Another shock was experiencing racism. Coming from a mainly black nation, she had never felt judged by the color of her skin before. The student worked to counteract these experiences by starting a diversity club at her high school.

Many Kenyans, however, are very happy with the education they are receiving in the United States. Schools in Kenya are often expensive and may not have the same standards as in America. Kenyan students in the United States are excited about the variety of subjects they can study and the freedom within the classroom. They feel there is great opportunity here.

Religion

Most Kenyans, about 76 percent, are Christian. Christianity was brought to Africa by European missionaries. The Kenyans already had a belief in a supreme being, so they had no trouble with the Christian idea of God. Many Kikuyu have converted to Christianity. The largest independent church in Kenya is the Church of Christ in Africa. It tries to help the poor in the cities by offering health care services and education.

Some American communities have enough Kenyans so that they have been able to establish their own churches. In other regions, a specific church service may be designated as a Kenyan service. Most Kenyans belong to Pentecostal or charismatic churches. While some are affiliated with established denominations, such as Seventh-Day Adventists, others are independent churches. The Kenyan Christian Fellowship in America is a national organization with local chapters that meet regularly. While their main emphasis is religious development, the members also focus on having fun and sharing the Kenyan culture with their children.

Some 18 percent of Kenyans still follow animism. This belief holds that every object has a soul or spirit that can influence people's lives. Through sacrifice and worship these spirits can be made happy. The Masai also believe in God, who lives above Mount Kilimanjaro. Some of the Kikuyu Tribe designate sacred places, quiet spots for prayer and reflection that may be marked with stone piles.

About 6 percent of Kenyans are Muslim. Most of Kenya's Muslims are from coastal areas that were easily reached by Arab traders. Many of the Somali community are Muslim, as well as Asians living in Kenya.

Holidays and Festivals

Christian holidays center on the church in both Kenya and America. Kenyan churches often have noisy, colorful Christmas services. An African band may play, and the church service may run all day long. People go outside and visit, returning to sing Christmas songs or listen to another sermon. In America, the congregations of Kenyan churches continue these traditions. Some adopt the American custom of decorating a Christmas tree.

To celebrate New Year's, Kenyans and Kenyan Americans alike often gather together as a family. On New Year's Eve, urban Kenyans like to go out for dinner and dancing. New Year's Day is usually spent in quiet reflection.

The two major Muslim holidays are Eid al-Fitr and Eid al-Adha. Eid al-Fitr comes at the end of the month of fasting. Eid al-Adha comes at the end of a pilgrimage, or holy journey, which ends at a mosque. Both are celebrated with feasts and special prayers, whether in Kenya or America.

The Arts

Samb Aminata of New York polishes one of the wooden sculptures from Kenya that she has for sale in her kiosk at the twenty-fourth annual Afro American Festival in Detroit, Michigan. The three-day festival celebrates African culture, music, art, and food.

In Kenya, music has a religious importance. It connects people to the spirit world. It is also a vital part of community events and family gatherings. Kenya has many traditional instruments, including drums, flutes, and lyres (stringed instruments). Drums and flutes often accompany storytellers, while lyres are usually played at festivals and to accompany singers. In America, one of the most popular Kenyan instruments is the mbira (em-BEER-uh). Also called a thumb piano, the mbira is a box with strips of metal fixed at one end. Each strip of metal is tuned to a different pitch. To produce a sound, the metal strips are flipped with the thumbs. The mbira is popular in America because it was so easy for immigrants to bring the small instrument with them.

Some dance troupes in the Washington, D.C., area have translated some of the traditional Kenyan dances into modern dance. These folk dances, once meant to ensure a good harvest or bring rain, are now performed in brightly colored, traditional dress for the enjoyment of the audience.

Kenyan immigrants have brought their storytelling and poetry traditions with them to America. Many Kenyan morality tales teach life lessons to the community. Most Kenyan folktales have animals for main characters. Kenyans are often encouraged to write down and preserve these traditional stories by their church leaders.

Food

Many Kenyans are very poor, and their diet has been limited by their income. When Kenyan immigrants arrive in America, the wide variety and easy availability of food in America are a delightful surprise. African markets in areas such as Washington, D.C., make it easy to find the ingredients needed for favorite dishes from home.

Traditionally, the Kenyan diet includes protein-rich beans, fruits and vegetables, and a variety of meats, including goat, beef, chicken, and fish. *Sukuma wiki,* a dish made from greens cooked in beef gravy, is served at many meals. *Ugali,* a dish resembling grits that is made from ground corn mixed with water or milk, often accompanies the *sukuma wiki.*

Papayas, pineapples, and mangoes are all traditional fruits eaten by Kenyans. But bananas are the most important and are served with most meals. They may be baked, boiled, steamed, fried, or roasted.

Kenyan food has been strongly influenced by the food and spices of its Indian immigrants. Indian bread–chapati–and fried dumplings–*samosas*–are sold in most towns and cities.

Kanga Cloth

For many Kenyan women, a holiday gives them a reason to buy a new *kanga*. A *kanga* is a colorful, rectangular cotton cloth that can be worn in many different ways, as a dress, a head cloth, a skirt, or a baby carrier. The first *kanga* cloth was made in the mid-1800s in Mombasa, Kenya, by sewing several large handkerchiefs together. Designs were then hand-printed onto the handkerchiefs in black. A sweet potato was used as a printing block. The black designs on the white cloth resembled the black and white guinea fowl known as *kanga*. Young girls are presented with their first *kanga* at puberty. A Swahili woman wears a special *kanga* at her wedding. The *kanga* may be placed over a woman's coffin at her death.

Kinolo (Steamed Banana Pudding)

1 cup water

1/2 cup cornmeal

6 ripe bananas, mashed

4 banana leaves

1 mango, peeled, pitted, and mashed

Combine the water, cornmeal, and bananas in a bowl. Separate the banana leaves. Take 1 leaf and place one-fourth of the banana mixture in the center. Wrap it up into a tidy, flat packet and tuck the ends underneath. Repeat with the remaining banana leaves.

Bring water in a steamer pan to a simmer. Place the packets on the steamer rack, cover, and steam for 30 minutes. Let stand at room temperature 30 minutes.

Unwrap each packet and cut each portion into 4 slices. Serve the mango on the side.

Note: Banana leaves can usually be found at Latin American markets. Corn husks, soaked in water for 10 minutes, may be substituted if you can't find banana leaves.

Makes four 6-inch packets.

Source: Soul and Spice:
African Cooking in the Americas
by Heidi Haughy Cusick

CHAPTER SIX

Koreans

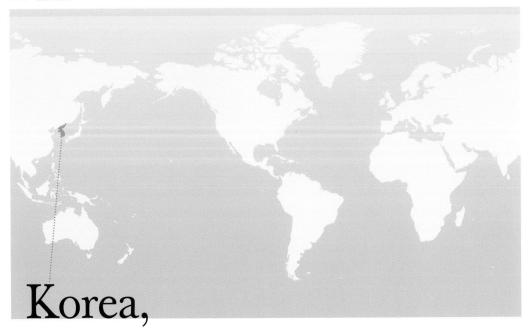

Korea,

once known as Chosen (CHO-sawn)–"The Land of the Morning Calm,"–is a major source of tension in eastern Asia today. The Korean *peninsula* extends south from China and Russia. Japan lies to the east. These three historical powers have had a tremendous impact on Korea's history. Since 1948, Korea has been divided into North and South Korea, two different countries with very different governments and *economies*.

A Quick Look Back

Over 2,000 years ago, wandering tribes of hunters, fishers, and farmers arrived on the Korean peninsula. These settlers created three kingdoms that fought for control through much of Korea's early history. The kingdoms were eventually united in the fourteenth century as the kingdom of Chosen. Chosen's culture was heavily influenced by the Buddhist religion and Confucian values of its neighbor, China.

For the next five hundred years, Chosen fought off attempted invasions by Japan and Manchuria (present-day northeastern China). Korean culture flourished, and Koreans believed that they needed nothing from other cultures. Chosen's desire for isolation was challenged in the late 1800s when foreign countries sought trading relationships with Korea, often by resorting to force. The Hermit Kingdom, as it became known, responded by closing its borders to everyone except China in 1866. Christianity was also outlawed at this time, but American missionaries continued to enter the country, preaching religion and democracy.

Japanese Control

China and Japan's struggle for power in Asia moved to the Korean peninsula when the Sino-Japanese War began in 1894. (*Sino* is a Latin prefix that refers to China.) Japan won the war within a year and soon occupied Korea. Japan officially took control of Korea in 1910.

By the 1930s, the Japanese had ordered Koreans to speak only Japanese, take Japanese names, and worship only at Japanese Shinto shrines. Some Koreans were shipped to Japan to work as slaves in coal mines and factories.

The Allied victory in World War II resulted in the removal of the Japanese from Korea, but not freedom for Koreans. The United States and the Soviet Union, allies during the war, were bitter enemies following the war. During the so-called Cold War, the Soviets encouraged the spread of *Communism* in *Third World* countries, while the United States supported forces fighting against Communism. One of these Cold War disputes took place in Korea.

The two superpowers, each fearing the other would take control of Korea, worked to influence the selection of the postwar Korean government. The Soviets supported Kim Il-Sung, a *Communist* leader in northern Korea who was pushing for a reform of land ownership laws. The United States backed nationalist groups in the south that wanted to restore Korea's original land laws, keeping most of the land in the hands of a wealthy few. Since they were unable to reach a compromise, they made a decision to split the country along the thirty-eighth parallel. Two new countries, Communist-led North Korea (Democratic People's Republic of Korea) and democratic South Korea (Republic of Korea), were established in 1948.

The Thirty-Eight Parallel

Parallels are the imaginary lines that encircle the globe in an east-west direction. They are parallel to the equator, which is how they get their name. The thirty-eighth parallel refers to the imaginary line that divides Korea in half at 38° latitude.

Two Koreas

By 1950, attempts by North Korea to extend its control into South Korea resulted in a civil war. Known as the Korean War, it became a battleground in the Cold War when the United Nations (UN) organized forces to resist the Soviet-backed North Korea. The United States sent many troops to support South Korea. China soon sent troops to support North Korea.

After three years of fighting, neither side had a victory. Korea was in ruins. Ongoing negotiations for peace finally resulted in an agreement on July 27, 1953. The agreement was signed by the UN, China, and North Korea, but South Korea's government never signed the agreement because it refused to acknowledge a divided Korea. Without a peace treaty signed, the two nations are still officially at war.

The DMZ

A *cease-fire* line, or demilitarized (dee-MIL-i-tur-*eyezd*) zone (DMZ), was established at the thirty-eighth parallel in 1953. Razor wire, land mines, and soldiers in watchtowers make this 151-mile-long (242 kilometers), 2.5-mile-wide (4 kilometers) strip the most heavily guarded border in the world. Almost 2 million troops are stationed along the DMZ, ready to resume the war in an instant if opposing forces cross the zone.

Korea Today

South Korea has grown rapidly since the Korean War. It has been helped by foreign aid, investments, and trade. This, in addition to South Koreans' creativity, hard work, and respect for education, has given South Korea a higher standard of living than North Korea. Until recently, however, South Korea has been troubled by a corrupt and repressive government.

In 1997, Kim Dae Jung was elected president. His work to promote a better relationship with North Korea won him the Nobel Peace Prize in 2000.

The people of North Korea still live in a *socialist dictatorship,* one of the few such states in existence since the fall of the Soviet Union. The state controls businesses, and there is little personal freedom. The standard of living for North Koreans remains low.

Currently under the leadership of Kim Jong Il, North Korea has been quietly experimenting with nuclear weapons.

In 2001, President George W. Bush named North Korea as one of the most troubling hot spots in the world.

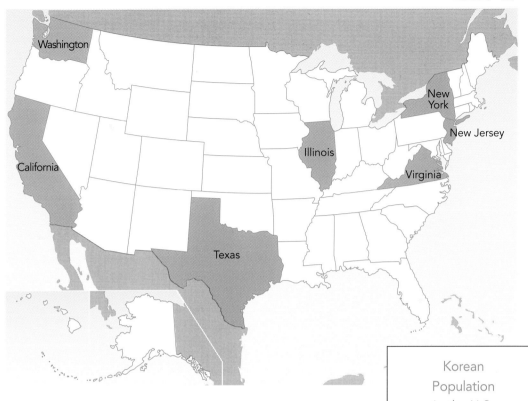

Coming to America

T he earliest immigrants from Korea arrived in Hawaii at the beginning of the twentieth century. Hawaii was a territory of the United States at that time, not yet a state. The Koreans came to work on the sugarcane plantations. When Japan invaded Korea in 1904, many Koreans fled from the cruelty of Japanese troops. Some made their way to Hawaii as well.

Other early immigrants came to the United States as "picture brides" between 1906 and 1923. Korean bachelors would arrange marriages with Korean women based on an exchange of photographs and letters.

By 1907, 1,000 Koreans had moved to the U.S. mainland, discouraged with the low-paying jobs on Hawaiian plantations. Most settled in California. Others traveled east, finding mining jobs in Utah, Colorado, and Wyoming.

Korean Population in the U.S.	
California	332,041
New York	145,537
New Jersey	62,804
Texas	49,586
Virginia	45,463
Illinois	42,725
Washington	41,641

Source: U.S. Census, 2000

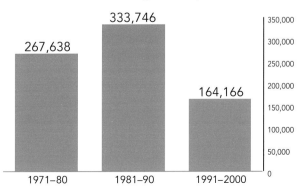

U.S./Korean Immigration by Decade

Source: Statistical Yearbook of the Immigration and Naturalization Service

San Francisco and Los Angeles had the largest Korean communities. Two towns in the San Joaquin Valley, Dinuba and Reedley, also drew the immigrants. There, they found work in vineyards and on fruit and vegetable farms. Agricultural workers were at a disadvantage, with little choice but to work for other landowners. They were unable to purchase and develop their own land because they were not allowed to become citizens, a prerequisite for owning land in California. (Until the 1950s, nonwhite immigrants were not allowed to become naturalized citizens.)

American cities offered few jobs for educated Koreans. They could be gardeners, janitors, housekeepers, restaurant workers, or railroad laborers. The racism and ignorance they experienced led many Koreans to start their own businesses. Korean-owned hotels sprang up in California and Washington. Some Korean immigrants started newspapers printed in Korean. Other Koreans opened groceries, bakeries, restaurants, barbershops, and laundries.

A *nativist* group called the Asiatic Exclusion League formed to pressure employers not to hire Asian workers. It also pressured the government not to allow any new immigrants from Asia into the country. The league members argued that Asians were too different from other Americans and would never be able to assimilate, or fit in, to American culture. The Asiatic Exclusion League was successful in its push for new restrictions. Legislation passed in 1907 prohibited Koreans and Japanese from *immigrating* to the mainland. In 1924, nearly all immigration from Asia was stopped.

Wartime Immigrants

Koreans in the United States became very involved in the war effort of World War II. This was remarkable since they faced ignorance from some Americans who did not know the difference between Korea and Japan. The Korean immigrants taught Japanese to American soldiers. They joined the U.S. Army and translated captured documents. They served as spies for the United States in Asia. Korean women joined the Red Cross and the men joined organizations designed to protect America. They bought defense bonds that helped pay for the war effort. In fact, Koreans in America—fewer than 10,000 people—bought more than $239,000 in bonds. The Koreans' commitment to winning the war earned them the respect of white America.

During the Korean War (1950–1953), American soldiers fought with South Korean troops against North Korea. They came to know the South Korean people. They met and married Korean women. These "war brides" were the first Korean immigrants to be legally allowed into the United States since 1924.

The McCarran-Walter Act in 1952 reopened America to Asian immigrants, even though it allowed only 100 immigrants from each country per year. In 1965, the Immigration and Nationality Act did away with these limits. The new law gave priority to immigrants whose skills and education were in demand in the United States. Thousands of South Korean doctors, nurses, and others with technical and scientific skills entered the United States. These newcomers, unlike most of the earlier Korean immigrants, came from upper-class families.

The 1965 law also allowed established immigrants to bring family members to America. Since 1972, most of the roughly 20,000 Koreans that immigrate each year have been sponsored by family members already living in the United States.

Many early Korean immigrants were from northern Korea. But since the end of the Korean War almost all immigrants have been from South Korea. Over 80 percent of Korean Americans are first-generation immigrants or the children of immigrants.

California governor Gray Davis, surrounded by members of the Korean community, signs a bill allowing Korean bakers to serve traditional, unrefrigerated, steamed rice cakes in the Koreatown area of Los Angeles. Previously, health officials had required the soft, chewy, bite-sized cakes to be refrigerated.

Nearly half of immigrants coming each year make their way to "Koreatown" in Los Angeles. This once-poor neighborhood has been revitalized by its 150,000 Korean

Americans. The borough of Queens in New York City has a majority of that city's 200,000 Korean Americans. Two-thirds of Korean Americans live in only five states–California, Hawaii, New York, Illinois, and New Jersey.

Spotlight on
CHAN HO PARK

Chan Ho Park, starting pitcher and relief pitcher for the Los Angeles Dodgers, was the first Korean to play in major league baseball. In his first appearance in 1994, he threw 95-mile-per-hour (152 kilometers) pitches and struck out two hitters.

Born in Kongju City, South Korea, in 1973, Park was recruited by the Dodgers to play in Los Angeles. He is only the fifth person of Asian descent to play in the major leagues.

Life in America

An independent spirit and tough-mindedness has allowed recent immigrants and second-generation Korean Americans to prosper. There are now Korean-language newspapers in cities like Atlanta, Seattle, and Chicago. Korean businesspeople are at the top of the grocery, dry-cleaning, and convenience store industries. Their children attend the best colleges and universities. Korean Americans have gained great success in their adopted country. However, gaps between generations and the pull of the two cultures, American and Korean, often result in a painful challenge as Korean Americans search for their identity.

Family

Korean American families differ from American families in their definition of good behavior. Strongly influenced by Confucian beliefs, Korean Americans believe that parents, children, and extended family should know how to act properly. Respect for elders sometimes motivates Koreans to sacrifice what they want for what the authority figures want. They do not understand the American belief in the individual and personal happiness.

The father is the traditional head of household. He makes the decisions for the whole family. He takes direction only from his own parents. The Korean wife is expected to obey her husband and her husband's parents. The Korean father also expects to choose his child's profession and marriage partner. Arranged marriages are still common between Korean Americans. Only about 15 percent of Korean Americans marry outside their *ethnic group*. However, this trend seems to be increasing for second-generation Korean Americans.

Korean women have a hard time reconciling Eastern and Western beliefs about the role of women in the home. In Korea, few women work outside the home. Once they are in the United States, however, up to 75 percent join the workforce. This trend, in the traditional Korean view, makes women more independent and less obedient. It also strains Korean marriages in America. The divorce rate for Korean immigrants who arrived after 1965 is higher than the national average.

Korean American children sometimes feel closer to American culture than their Korean roots. They are influenced by movies, television, and music. Their English, because of this media exposure, is usually better than their parents' English. Their grandparents may not speak any English at all. Some second-generation children only speak "Kitchen Korean." This means they only understand about half of what they hear. This language barrier in the home creates another tension between the generations. As a result, many Korean American families send their children to Korea to learn traditional culture and values.

Work

From the turn of the twentieth century to today, from plantation workers to scientists and doctors, Americans of Korean descent have helped build the United States.

The Immigration Act of 1965 paved the way for Korean professionals to make the move to the United States. Doctors and nurses poured into the United States, already trained. Sometimes it took a while before these professionals could receive their licenses to practice medicine. While waiting, they often took other jobs in the health care profession, such as x-ray technicians.

Did you know?

Korean Americans own 135,571 businesses, employing more than 333,000 people.

Korean Americans are among the most successful of immigrant entrepreneurs (people who start their own business). They own markets, groceries, and dry-cleaning businesses in New York City, Los Angeles, and other large cities. Korean American shop owners put in long hours, like many immigrant groups before them. As employers, taxpayers, and consumers, Korean Americans have helped rebuild many poor neighborhoods.

School

Many non–Asian Americans believe that all Korean American children study hard, do well at math, play a musical instrument, and obey their parents. But of course this is not the case. This belief can lead to trouble at school.

Some Korean American students feel the pressure of living up to the very high expectations of parents and society. They are encouraged to keep quiet about their troubles and not show weakness by asking for help. Some drop out, take drugs, or get into trouble because they think they have failed when they do not get good grades.

Spotlight on
MARGARET CHO

Comedian Margaret Cho performs to a packed house at the Sound-Capitol Performing Arts Center in York, Pennsylvania. The daughter of Korean immigrants has also performed at Carnegie Hall in New York.

Margaret Cho was born on December 5, 1968, to Seung-Hoon Cho and his wife Young-Hie. They had come to America in 1964 to continue their college education. After graduating from the High School for Performing Arts in San Francisco, Margaret Cho attended college briefly, majoring in theater. Frustrated with the acting parts available to Asian American women, she turned to stand-up comedy. Two years and over 300 concerts later, Cho won the American Comedy Award for Female Comedian in 1994.

That same year, Cho became the first Asian American of Korean descent to produce and star in her own television series. It was called *All-American Girl.*

Religion

About 65 percent of the Koreans in America are Christians. Christians follow the teachings of Jesus Christ. In America, there is one Korean church for every 350 Korean Americans.

Korean American Christian churches offer social and cultural support for Korean immigrants—a place to socialize with those who share their heritage. On a typical Sunday, Koreans attend an early morning church service and then spend the rest of the day participating in meetings and cultural programs at the church. The churches also offer language classes and a place to practice English skills throughout the week.

Koreans also bring their Confucian and Buddhist beliefs with them to America. Confucianism promotes relationships that result in an orderly society. Respect for authority, education, and elders are all important Confucian values.

Most Korean Buddhists follow Pure Land Buddhism. Their goal is to reach an enlightened state, from which they can help others. They believe that they can achieve this goal by demonstrating love, compassion, and patience toward others and by living a simple life.

Holidays and Festivals

Koreans in America celebrate their arts, culture, and history through Asian American community festivals as well as festivals that are unique to Korea.

New Year's Day

For Koreans in America as in Korea, New Year's Day falls on two dates. The first New Year's Day is shared with the West— January 1. Many immigrants in America continue the Korean tradition of greeting the first sunrise of the year. The rest of the day is filled with dancing, singing, and drumming. In some American communities, Korean Americans carry on the tradition of Ji-shin-bal-ki. This event takes place during the first fifteen days of January, *p'ungmul* players (traditional actors) visit businesses in the Korean community to extend wishes for a prosperous new year.

Members of a Korean dance troupe from Kemyong University in South Korea attend a presentation by the Korean American Cultural Foundation at the Texas Korean War Veterans Memorial on the state capitol grounds in Austin, Texas.

The second celebration is the traditional Korean New Year, or Lunar New Year. It falls on the first day of the first month of the lunar calendar. The first three days of the Lunar New Year are called *sol-nal* (SOL-nal). In preparation for the new year, people clean their houses and pay their bills. On the first day of the New Year, everyone dresses in new clothes. Traditional families serve a thick beef broth for breakfast. Eating this broth ensures that you turn one year older. Traditionally, all Koreans turn one year older on New Year's Day.

Next, the family honors its *ancestors,* offering them incense and food. Children then make formal bows to their parents to show how grateful they are for their parents' care. This respect for parents is called filial piety and is a very important character trait for Koreans. When the visiting begins, people visit the oldest relatives first to show respect for elders. After bowing, they receive gifts and advice from their elders. Then, they visit other family and friends.

Most Korean Americans celebrate the Korean New Year, maintaining many of the cultural traditions of their ancestors. However, a new aspect is often added—the sharing of the Korean culture with the larger community. In large cities, a parade may be the highlight of the festivities. Festivals introduce traditional foods, music, games, and crafts. Korean dance troupes perform centuries-old dances.

Tae-Bo-Rum is the Great Moon Festival of the Lunar New Year. It falls on the first day of the first month. People gather on a hill and wait for the moon to rise. Koreans believe that catching sight of the first full moon as it rises will bring good luck for the coming year.

Other Holidays

Cities with a large Korean American population, such as Los Angeles, host Korean Independence Day parades on August 15. These events celebrate the end of Japanese rule in Korea.

In spring, on the eighth day of the fourth lunar month, Buddhists everywhere celebrate Buddha's birthday, known as the Feast of the Lanterns. In America, the birthday celebrations often take place at Buddhist temples or community centers on a weekend in May. Colorful paper lanterns symbolizing hope decorate the temples.

The first day of the celebration often includes discussions and presentations that promote a peaceful and just society.

Vegetarian feasts generally cap off the evening, along with traditional music. The second day of the festival is devoted to religious ceremonies. Meditation services begin the morning; then each individual is invited to "bathe," or pour water over, a statue of the baby Buddha. Children attending the ceremony are blessed by the monks.

While lantern parades are common in Korea, American celebrations typically end with a lantern and chanting service. Individuals dedicate the paper lanterns, marking a commitment to gain spiritual strength, asking for Buddha's blessing, or remembering a loved one. They write their dedications on slips of paper and attach them to the lanterns, which are lit during the evening ceremony.

In autumn, Ch'usok (CHOO-soak) Day, or the Harvest Moon Festival, is a day of thanksgiving for Koreans. To prepare for the festival, Koreans buy wine and fruits such as dates, chestnuts, and persimmons. One of the favorite treats of this day is *Kkaegangjong* (KAE-ghang-jung). These are small cakes made from sesame seeds. At the end of the celebration, people like to sit under the moon's light and recite or make up poetry. They believe the moon inspires them to be artistic.

The Arts

Many Korean American organizations teach children and adults traditional folk arts. Korean musicians and dancers begin with a story. Then they improvise the music and dance as they go along, creating a new dance every time. Some of the art forms that are popular in America are described below.

• *P'ansori* (pahn-so-ri). The *p'ansori* performer tells complex, adventurous tales using songs and gestures as well as speech. He or she is accompanied by a drummer. A raspy voice is preferred.

• *P'ungmul/samulnori* (poong-mool, sah-mool-nor-ee). Also known as a farmers' band, these groups often entertained at festivals and puppet shows. In America, *p'ungmul* usually includes acrobats and actors as well as many drummers. Modern professional percussion bands with four musicians are called *samulnori*. In America, both groups often include women, something that was forbidden in Korea.

• *Salp'uri* (sahl-poo-ri). This traditional dance is very popular with Korean Americans. Most Korean American girls are expected to learn traditional Korean dances, which teach about heritage and etiquette.

Cultural Differences

Many Korean Americans are not as comfortable smiling as Americans are. They believe that if nothing is funny, then there is nothing to smile about. They think it is foolish to smile without a good reason. So they do not always smile when they meet someone. Looking someone directly in the eyes is also considered bad manners.

To show affection or to touch in public is considered bad manners in Korean culture. A simple gesture, like a man taking a woman's hand, is considered embarrassing. This is why Korean American storekeepers do not drop change into a customer's hand. They usually put the money on the counter for the customer to pick up.

Some Americans have been offended by these differences. In south Los Angeles, where tensions run high between African Americans and Korean shop owners, cultural differences like these have caused misunderstandings.

Food

Korean food is gaining popularity in the United States. Its healthy ingredients and spicy flavors attract many diners. Even places like Atlanta, Houston, and Milwaukee, which don't have substantial Korean populations, have at least one Korean restaurant. A typical restaurant serves rice, soup, and the hot, spicy, pickled vegetable dish called kimchi (KIM-chee).

As winter approaches, Koreans make enough kimchi to last through the cold months ahead, a tradition still practiced because in earlier times people could not buy the ingredients for kimchi during winter. Koreans prepare kimchi and store it in crockery pots that, traditionally, were buried up to their necks in the yard.

Small dishes called *pan chan* are put in the middle of the table for everyone to eat out of using chopsticks. *Pan chan* includes tofu, spinach and bean sprouts, a vegetable pancake, and a kind of pudding made out of bean paste.

Most Korean meals include several main dishes with vegetables and a meat, like salted fish or barbecued beef ribs.

Recipe

Baechu Kimchi (Cabbage Pickle)

Kimchi is served at most meals in Korea. There are many types of kimchi. This type, made from cabbage, is probably the best known and most popular.

1 large Chinese cabbage (21/2–3 pounds), cut into 2-inch-wide slices

1/2 cup salt

6 green onions, green and white parts, finely chopped

3 cloves garlic, minced

2 tablespoons Korean red pepper powder or 1 tablespoon cayenne

1/4 teaspoon grated fresh ginger root

1 tablespoon sugar

3/4 cup hot water

Wash the chopped cabbage. Drain and sprinkle with salt; let stand in a colander for 2 hours. Rinse with cold water and squeeze out excess liquid. Place cabbage in a large bowl.

Add the onions, garlic, Korean red pepper powder, ginger, and sugar to the cabbage. Toss and mix until cabbage is well coated.

Pack the cabbage mixture in a crock or a large glass jar. Pour the hot water into the bowl that held the cabbage mixture, and swish around to gather any remaining seasonings. Pour into the jar of packed cabbage. Cover the jar with a tight lid and place in a cool room for 2 days before refrigerating. (This will allow the fermentation process to begin and intensify the flavors.)

Refrigerate at least 24 hours before serving. Makes 2 quarts.

Source: Flavors of Korea: Delicious Vegetarian Cuisine *by Deborah Coultrip-Davis and Young Sook Ramsay*

CHAPTER SEVEN

Laotians

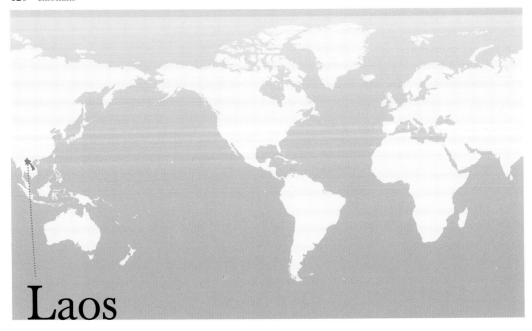

Laos

(lous) is located in the center of Indochina, the *peninsula* between India and China. Thailand and Myanmar (formerly Burma) border Laos on the west, Cambodia lies to the south, and Vietnam curls around Laos to the east. It is a small, narrow country, about two-thirds the size of Vietnam, but slightly larger than Cambodia. Laos, Vietnam, and Cambodia are often referred to as French Indochina because France once colonized the region.

The people of Laos are a mix of about seventy tribal groups that had their beginnings in India, Thailand, and China. The largest *ethnic group* is the Lao, who are related to the Thai people. Other major groups are the Hmong and

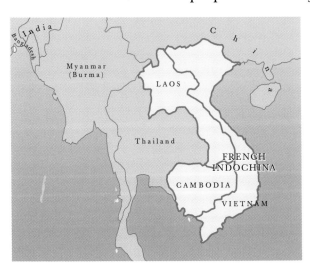

Mien tribes. The Lao, who consider themselves a different race from the Hmong and Mien, are the major political force in Laos. They live along the Mekong River in the lowlands. The Hmong and the Mien *emigrated* from China and live in the mountains of Laos. The name "Laotian" is used in this book to refer to all three groups: Lao, Hmong, and Mien.

A Quick Look Back

In its earliest days, Laos was a land of scattered tribes and kingdoms. In the mid-1300s, this loose collection of tribes was united into Lan Xang, or the "land of a million elephants," by a leader named Fa Ngum. The kingdom of Lan Xang was peaceful until the mid-1500s when it was forced to defend itself against invasions by neighboring Siam and Burma. Finally, in 1637, a prince named Souligna Vongsa was able to bring peace to the country. He restored the power of Lan Xang and strengthened its borders. He made treaties with Annam (Vietnam) and Siam. He built many temples and the country prospered. European traders arriving in 1641 were surprised at the wealth and accomplishments of the kingdom.

After Souligna Vongsa's death in 1695, a fight for power among his successors split Lan Xang into three kingdoms. Siam, Burma, and Annam relaunched their fight for control of the region. By 1778, Siam had gained control over all three kingdoms.

French Indochina

The French were interested in controlling parts of Indochina because they were searching for inland routes to China. In 1864, they took over Vietnam and Cambodia. Siam tried to fight the French, but wound up giving them Lan Xang. The French began drawing new borders between the countries without considering the ethnic makeup of the people. Years later, however, conflicts between the ethnic groups contributed to unrest and *rebellions* in the region. In the new French *protectorate,* Lan Xang became Laos, Siam became Thailand, and Cochin China, Annam, and Tonkin became Vietnam. (A *protectorate* is a relationship in which a strong country agrees to protect a smaller country or region in return for some degree of control over the smaller country's affairs.)

During the early years of French rule, Laos enjoyed peace. The local rulers remained in office, and the French ruled through them. France built a few hospitals and schools, but World War I and the economic depression of the 1930s slowed any civil works programs.

During World War II, the Japanese occupied Indochina. They forced the Laotian king, Sisavang Vong, to declare the country's independence from France and accept Japanese assistance in running the country.

In 1945, after Japan's surrender at the end of the war, France resumed its protectorate, supported by the U.S. government, and French officials returned to Laos.

Although the French regained control of Cambodia, Laos, and Vietnam, they had to fight to remain in power. This conflict, which lasted until 1954, involved all three *colonies* and was called the First Indochina War. During this time, the French agreed to negotiate, giving Laotians more control over the government. In 1949, Laos was declared an independent country within the French Union.

French paratroopers operate on the Plain of Jars in Laos during the Indochina War in 1953. They were fighting the Vietminh Communist army.

Many people wanted full independence. They formed a group called Pathet Lao (PAHT-uht lou), or Lao State, and allied themselves with the Vietnamese *Communist* liberation group in North Vietnam called the Vietminh (Vee-et-MIN). The fighting intensified until, in 1954, the French agreed to peace negotiations.

Independence for Laos

Peace negotiations for the First Indochina War were held in Geneva, Switzerland, with United Nations Security Council members from France, the United States, the Soviet Union, and other major countries in attendance. They reached an agreement, known as the Geneva Accords, that was signed by France, Laos, Cambodia, and representatives from North and South Vietnam. Laos and Cambodia were given full independence from France. Vietnam was divided in half. North Vietnam was given to the Communist forces of the Vietminh under Ho Chi Minh (ho chee min). South Vietnam was set up as a democracy and backed by Western forces. An election scheduled for 1956 would reunite the country under one government.

Power Struggles

The newly independent Kingdom of Laos was placed under the leadership of the royal government, which had cooperated with the French. Initially, two northern provinces were placed under the control of the Pathet Lao. By 1957, the Pathet Lao and royal leaders had agreed to form a coalition (partnership) government that combined the Kingdom of Laos and the two Pathet Lao provinces.

The United States was worried about the increasing power of the Pathet Lao. Believing that the Royal Lao Army was the only group strong enough to fend off Communist-backed threats to the government, the United States provided military support and money for salaries to the army. The United States also provided weapons to the Hmong, who helped fight against the Pathet Lao and North Vietnamese. But, in 1959, the Pathet Lao took control of the northern part of Laos with support from the North Vietnamese and overthrew the government.

Fighting continued as the civil war in northern Laos lasted for the next eight years. U.S. and North Vietnamese–backed groups fought for control. Finally, with the United States beginning to withdraw troops from Vietnam, negotiations for peace began once more. The negotiations ended with a cease-fire agreement. A new coalition government was installed in 1974, giving equal representation to all factions.

In April 1975, South Vietnam fell under the control of North Vietnamese troops. That same year, Cambodia fell to Communist Khmer Rouge forces. With no U.S. troops left in Southeast Asia, Laos fell to the Pathet Lao.

Under Communist Rule

The Pathet Lao seized power over all Laos and declared it a *socialist republic,* the Lao People's Democratic Republic. Many people were sent to camps for "reeducation." This meant that they were forced to learn the new Communist government's beliefs against their will. An estimated 30,000 Hmong people, including women and children, were executed in retaliation for the Hmong's role as resistance fighters against the Pathet Lao and North Vietnamese Army. Over 175,000 people fled the country during the late 1970s and early 1980s. First, they made their way to refugee camps in Thailand. From there, they thought they would go to the West and the United States.

The new Pathet Lao government enforced Communist policies which resulted in major economic problems in the late 1970s and early 1980s. In an effort to reverse the decline, the government opened up the country to foreign investors. It also moved to a market-based *economy,* which meant that prices were determined by supply and demand rather than by the government.

By the late 1980s, the economy was beginning to grow again. But Laos's main trading partner and source of financial aid—the Soviet Union—was dissolving. Vietnam began withdrawing its troops as well. Laos worked to renew relationships with foreign countries.

A new *constitution,* without any reference to socialism or Communism, was written in 1991. In 1995, the United States lifted its ban on trade with Laos. Even though Laos has more freedom than it did, the Pathet Lao has managed to keep power.

A street vendor walks past Laotian soldiers who are guarding the Laos seventh congress being held in the Laos Cultural Center building in Vientiane, Laos.

Laos Today

Conditions for the common people in Laos have improved but only in small ways. The Soviets helped the Laotian government build a modern hospital. But Laos has only one doctor for every 3,500 people. The infant death rate is the highest in the world. Most people live only into their early fifties. Hunger and poverty are still a major problem.

The Lao People's Revolutionary Party (LPRP) has set some education standards for its people. Many more Laotians are attending secondary schools and, the literacy rate is rising. Most Laotians want a better education. They see that the future of Laos is tied to education.

Laos is still one of the world's most underdeveloped countries. It remains predominantly agricultural. The LPRP is trying to build more factories and manufacturing plants, however.

Outside forces threaten the future of Laos and its political stability. Laos and Thailand and Myanmar still fight over territory as they have for centuries. Tensions between China and Indochina continue as well.

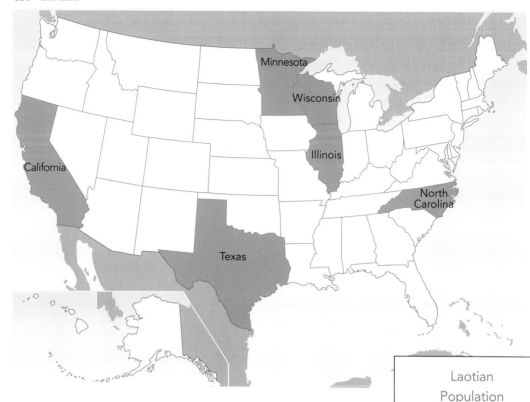

Laotian Population in the U.S.

California	87,446
Wisconsin	47,848
Minnesota	34,711
North Carolina	16,139
Illinois	6,748
Texas	6,198

Source: U.S. Census, 2000

Coming to America

T he Laotians' journey to America is different in many respects from that of other Asian immigrants. The Laotians came to the United States as refugees, fleeing war in their own country rather than seeking economic opportunity or education. The Laotians had to leave their homes quickly, taking little or nothing with them except their memories.

From Laos to Thailand

When the Pathet Lao took control, Laotians who had supported the United States intervention had to run for their lives. The Hmong and the Mien were a major target for the Pathet Lao's anger. Many thousands fled to Thailand.

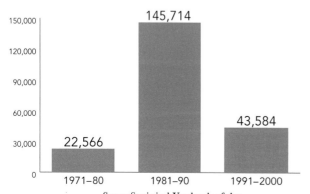

U.S./Laotian Immigration by Decade

Decade	Immigration
1971–80	22,566
1981–90	145,714
1991–2000	43,584

Source: Statistical Yearbook of the Immigration and Naturalization Service

The journey to the Thai border was dangerous and had to be made as quickly and as quietly as possible. Small children had to walk 15 to 20 miles (24 to 32 kilometers) or more through dense jungle. Adults carried food, whatever goods they could save from their homes, and babies. Many elderly people and children died on the way. Some people were caught by the Pathet Lao and tortured to death or shot.

Reaching the refugee camps did not end the struggle for survival. Although church and aid groups from around the world supplied food and tried to maintain sanitary conditions, the camps were dirty and filled with starving refugees. Thieves stole what little the refugees had left. Some of the refugees had to stay in the camps for five years or longer.

Arrival in the United States

Many church and aid groups in the United States acted as sponsors for Laotian refugees who were waiting in the camps of Thailand. Sponsors are people who agree to help refugees adjust to life in America and to help them financially if necessary. Some Americans became sponsors because they felt that they owed the Laotians something for their support of America in the Vietnam War. Others were simply moved by the suffering of the refugees.

By the end of the 1980s, about 140,000 Laotian refugees had resettled in the United States. They represented three main ethnic groups. About 70,000 were Lao, 60,000 were Hmong, and 10,000 were Mien.

Today, there are more than 250,000 Laotians in the United States. About 90,000 are Hmong, and about 12,000 are Mien. The rest are of Lao descent. Many ethnic Laotian communities can be found across the United States. Wisconsin and Minnesota each have large, active Hmong communities, but one of the largest is in the Fresno, California, area. California is also home to most of the Mien and Lao.

Life in America

Laotians who were granted permission to come to America were usually in their new homes in Minneapolis, Minnesota, or another American city three days after they left the refugee camps. But many of the refugees, especially the Hmong and Mien, had grown up in

Giant Jars

In northwestern Laos is a flat expanse of land called the Tran Ninh Plateau. Near the center of this plateau is a plain covered with grass and a few trees. This is the Plain of Jars, named for the giant stone jars, shaped like beehives, that dot the plain.

Each of the stone jars, weighing 4,000 to 6,000 pounds (1.8 to 2.7 metric tons) and standing 3 to 9 feet (1 to 3 meters) tall, was carved from a single piece of stone. The stone is not native to the area. Archaeologists are puzzled. They do not know who carved the jars, how the jars were moved to the plain, or what their purpose was. The jars come from a long-vanished *civilization*, so we may never know whether they were used as burial urns, for storage, or for some other purpose.

remote mountain villages. The conveniences of the twentieth century were all new to them. They had to learn the most basic things, such as how to turn the lights on and off, use a stove, and fill the bathtub with water.

Many Laotians have found American *culture* hard to understand. The Lao, however, have adjusted fairly easily to American cities and culture. They had lived in large cities in Laos and were educated. They also have a written language that has much in common with the Thai language. This has made it less difficult for them to learn to read and write English.

In contrast, many Hmong and Mien have had trouble adjusting to life in America. Once farmers in small villages, most now live in inner-city neighborhoods. Their language had no written form, but now they must learn basic reading skills to survive. The elderly, who were once honored and obeyed, find themselves dependent upon children when dealing with day-to-day life in America. Many of the older Hmong and Mien refugees have experienced depression. Living in often violent, urban neighborhoods, they are afraid to leave their homes. Neighbors call them the "invisible people."

Lao, Hmong, and Mien people have had to struggle against American ignorance about their identity. Americans often think that Laotians are Chinese. Americans know little about Laotians and their history. This ignorance hurts the Laotians, who lost so much by helping America in its fight against North Vietnam.

Family

Laotians come from mainly rural areas. In their villages, people depended upon each other. Many generations of a family lived in one home. In the desperate rush to the refugee camps, many families were separated. In America they have had to deal with loneliness that they never knew in Laos.

The changing structure of the family has caused problems as well. Traditionally, male leaders of the extended family were consulted before any major decision was made. The family leaders settled conflicts and made sure everyone was taken care of. In America, family leaders do not have as much power. They may not speak English well or understand enough about how American society works to make sure everyone gets the help they need. A family leader may even live in another state or country. People in the younger generation, those who grew up in America, are emerging as the new leaders.

In many cases, these new advocates are women, who would never have held such positions in Laos. This empowerment of women represents a major change in family roles. Traditionally, the Laotian husband is the head of the family and is responsible for supporting his wife and children. Laotian women have been wives and mothers who worked in the home. In an effort to make enough money to support their families, many Laotian women in the United States have now started working outside the home.

Children of Laotian immigrants, the members of the Whyteshadows band play Latin music and contemporary rock and roll. The new generation of Hmong Americans in California's San Joaquin Valley are trying to appeal to their audience's ever-changing tastes.

The inability to support the family, as well as other factors, has caused depression in many Hmong men. Since 1988, over 100 Hmong men between the ages of thirty and fifty have died from a condition called Hmong Sudden Death Syndrome after showing signs of severe depression. Health care workers remain puzzled by the condition.

Like most teenagers, Laotian American youth have trouble establishing their independence from their parents. They are caught between the traditional values of their parents and American values of individualism and independent thinking. Girls, especially, are caught in the trap of conflicting values. They are taught through school and the media that girls can be anything they want to be. At home, though, the girls are still expected to follow strict rules of behavior and to spend their free time helping with housework and watching younger siblings. They are encouraged to follow tradition and marry at a young age, typically fourteen. Teenage girls often rebel by skipping school or running away from home.

While Laotian boys also have conflicts with their parents, they are allowed many more privileges. They do not usually have chores to do at home, so they may be allowed to socialize with their friends after school or in the evenings. Even so, the number of Laotian boys who run away from home or join street gangs is increasing as well.

Ceremonies and rituals that are important to the Laotian family and culture are often difficult to observe in America. In Laos, wedding ceremonies last more than a week. But in America, Laotians may not have enough money to have a traditional wedding. They have also learned that the noise of a traditional wedding will lead to complaints from the neighbors, so they have had to adapt their traditions.

Dabs

Telling Hmong parents that their baby is pretty is an invitation to disaster. Many believe that such a compliment draws the attention of evil spirits called *dabs* to the child. The baby is then in great danger because a *dab* might steal the baby's life-soul, which ensures health and happiness. It is for this same reason that Hmong babies are often dressed in brightly colored hats. They fool the *dabs* into believing that the child is really a flower.

Funerals are also very different in America. A traditional Hmong funeral lasts three days and is usually held at home. Specially trained musicians play music for each part of the ceremony. Men trained in the funeral ceremony are the only ones who can conduct it properly, but few of these men are in America. Funerals also call for ritual sacrifice of animals such as chickens, which presents great difficulty in America.

Many Lao, Mien, and Hmong people wonder if they will be able to keep their beliefs and their culture for very long in the United States. They are afraid their children will forget their languages. Many children have only known American culture, and they see their parents as old-fashioned and anxious. Since the Mien and Hmong languages were not written down, they are in great danger of being lost.

Work

Most Laotians were rice farmers. When they did not farm, they would hunt and fish for food. These skills do not help them in America, since they now live in crowded urban neighborhoods. Without basic English skills, they have found it difficult to get jobs. The Hmong and Mien have no written language. Reading maps and street signs is strange to them, which makes it hard to go to job interviews. Many are on welfare or working at low-wage jobs. Some Mien and Hmong sell crafts or do yard- or house-work. Within apartment complexes, some trade for goods as they did in Laos. In some cities, their unemployment rate is as high as 60 percent. Many Hmong have tried farming in Minnesota and California, but the kind of farming they did back in Laos does not work very well in the American climate. Also, they have discovered that owning land and farming are expensive in the United States.

A Hmong farmer poses in a plot of farmland he cultivates in California. Hmong farmers are lobbying for state aid to help them buy land and farm equipment.

Traditionally, Laotian women worked in the home and cared for the children. In America, however, they have begun working outside the home to help support their families. Some women continue the tradition of fine embroidery, selling pieces at community fairs or shops.

Most second- and third-generation Laotians are moving into professions such as law, medicine, and teaching. Some are beginning restaurants and other small businesses. Family and community *networks* are helpful to these small business owners.

School

Laotian parents realize that education is the key to their children's success in America. But they often have trouble encouraging their children's education because of their own lack of

English. They may not be able to help with homework, communicate with teachers, or participate in parent-teacher associations.

Communication problems also affect students in the classroom. For example, teachers expect students to speak up and ask questions if they don't understand an assignment. Laotian students often think that the teacher has given them all the information they are going to get. Not fully understanding assignments can lead to poor grades and discouragement in school. The truancy, or skipping school, of many Laotian students is related to these differences in communication.

In spite of these problems, younger Laotians are making the adjustment to American culture. They are literate in English and continue their education through college. In Providence, Rhode Island, about 90 percent of Laotian children go on to college. In St. Paul, Minnesota, about 80 percent go to college.

Like other Asian groups before them, Laotian students have experienced racism. They are called names and teased for being different. Some feel too afraid to confront the ignorance of their schoolmates. Others come to a breaking point and stand up to the name callers.

Cultural Confusion

Traditional Hmong have many taboos, or actions that are prohibited. When Americans are unaware of these taboos, they risk offending people without meaning to. Among the taboos are patting a baby's head, shaking hands, and looking into the eyes of an older person, all things that are commonplace in America.

Religion

Buddhism spread through Laos in the thirteenth century and was the official religion for over 700 years. When the Pathet Lao came to power in 1975, religion was banned. Despite the efforts of the ruling Communist Party, Buddhism remains an important belief in Laos today. Theravada, a traditional form of Buddhism, is the foundation for the values of most people of Laotian descent. Laotians in America have easily adapted their worship practices in America. Most cities with large Asian populations have a Buddhist temple. If a temple is not available, Laotian Buddhists may gather to worship in a community building or home.

Other Laotians practice *animism* (AN-uh-*miz*-um), or spirit worship. Animists believe that all things have spirits that are linked to a specific place. These spirits have great influence, good and bad, on the everyday lives of the people. Poor health or bad harvests are believed to be the result of an angry spirit.

To set things right, the local shaman (SHAY-man), or priest, prays to the spirits and offers sacrifices that will make the spirits happy. Laotian animists in America have had difficulty practicing their traditions. The move to America has separated the Laotians from the spirits that they used to call on for help. Many of the rituals require time that just isn't available in the American workweek. But perhaps more importantly, many Laotians lost confidence in their traditional religions during the resettlement process, through their contact with Christian organizations and individuals.

Holidays and Festivals

The first big celebration for a Laotian is a naming ceremony. Traditionally held three days after the child's birth, it is often held much later in America because the family has to save enough money to hold a "soul-calling" feast for family and friends. Until this ceremony is held, the child is not considered a full member of the human race. During the ceremony, rituals are performed to make sure that the chosen name is a good one. Strings may be tied around one of the baby's wrists by the parents and elders. These strings tie the soul to the child's body. Regardless of their chosen name, most children will be called by a nickname. They may change their name several times during their lifetime to reflect changes in their lives or to fool evil spirits.

Two girls dress in traditional Hmong clothes at the Hmong New Year celebration in Merced, California. The celebration has been held annually since the early 1980s.

The celebration of the New Year is eagerly anticipated by all Laotians. Its importance in America, however, represents the feeling of pride that the Lao and Hmong have in their traditions and heritage. These traditions provide meaning and security for older immigrants who remember such celebrations from their childhood. And they encourage second-generation Laotian Americans to learn more about the Lao and Hmong cultures.

For the Lao, the new year traditionally begins at the end of the dry season in Laos, in April. The date is determined by Buddhist monks according to star charts and the signs of the zodiac. People sweep out their houses in order to clean them of any bad spirits. The celebration traditionally lasts three days.

On the first day of the New Year holiday, Buddhist monks clean the holy statues and pictures in the temple with holy water. People take holy water home with them to purify their homes as well. Prayer mounds are built from sand or stones. Prayer flags with prayers and wishes written on them are planted in the mounds.

The second day is a celebration of family and friends. They gather to welcome the New Year and the return of all the souls, one for each part of the human body. White threads are tied around each person's wrist, and people exchange wishes for good luck and good health. People give offerings to Buddhist monks and enjoy demonstrations of traditional music and dance.

Traditionally, the final day of the Lao New Year features a parade. This is not always possible in America, where Lao communities are small. Throughout the celebration, people splash water on one another as a sign of good luck.

The Hmong New Year is celebrated toward the end of the year, usually late November. In America, the New Year is often celebrated around Thanksgiving. Traditionally, the New Year rituals honor ancestors. While the traditional celebration lasts anywhere from three days to a month and a half, American versions may be held on a weekend. Hmong people gather to share their traditional food and dances. Just as in Laos, the New Year provides an opportunity for young people to get acquainted and possibly meet their future spouses.

The Arts

Laotians have a traditional form of theater that includes dances with costumes and masks. Some dances show scenes from Laotian history, while others are performed to please the spirit world. Because of India's influence in Laotian history, dancers also may perform a story from an Indian epic, the *Ramayana*. One folk dance that is danced by both boys and girls is the *lamvong*. The complicated arm and hand movements express love, but the dancers do not touch. They look straight ahead throughout the dance.

Laotian musicians play a popular instrument called the *khene,* a reed pipe made of bamboo sticks tied together. Each stick of bamboo is cut to a different length to produce different notes. Another traditional bamboo instrument is the *nang-nat.* This is like a xylophone and is played with a small mallet.

Another Laotian art form is the shadow play. Silhouettes of puppets are cast onto a cloth screen that is hung between the performers and the audience. These paper silhouette puppets act out folk tales and religious stories.

Hmong Needlework

Intricate figures stitched and appliquéd onto fabric tell the story of the Hmong's journey to freedom. Traditional designs decorate belts, pillow covers, and wall hangings. This is the art of story cloths and *paj ntaub* (pan-doa).

Hmong women are known for their exquisite sewing skills. In their villages in Laos, part of their status was based on how well they sewed. *Paj ntaub* features traditional geometric designs, sewn with strips of cloth and tiny stitches. When the Hmong fled to the refugee camps in Thailand, a new art form emerged. Hmong men used their idle time to draw pictures showing their escape from the villages, planes flying overhead, soldiers shooting at them, and boats waiting to take them across the river to Thailand. The women translated these illustrations onto cloth and embroidered them.

Few of the younger Hmong women are learning *paj ntaub*. They say it is too time-consuming and doesn't make enough money. As the beautiful story cloths and *paj ntaub* become scarcer, their value has increased. Many museums are now collecting these pieces of the Hmong culture, afraid that the complex craft is dying out.

This paj ntaub *storytelling quilt was created by May Chao Lor in Green Bay, Wisconsin. The Hmong have had a written language for only about fifty years, so traditionally they used quilts to document folklore and history.*

Food

When Laotians arrived in American, the food and utensils were a shock. Most Laotian refugees were used to eating with their fingers. Others, like the Mien, were used to eating with chopsticks.

Laotian food is a mixture of hot and sweet tastes. Every meal includes rice, the most important food in the Laotian diet. Sticky rice is served in one bowl that everyone eats from. Diners use their fingers to roll the rice into balls. Then they dip the balls in different sauces. Coconut milk is served with spicy meals to cool and sweeten the hot taste of peppers.

Nam pa, or fish sauce, is a favorite flavoring. This thick paste, made by straining water through salted, dried fish, is served with many different dishes. *Nam pa,* fresh fish, eggs, and chicken provide protein in the Laotian diet.

Recipe

Yam Kai Tom (Boiled Chicken Salad)

6 ounces boneless chicken breast

2 garlic cloves, thinly sliced

5 small shallots, thinly sliced

2 small fresh red chilies, finely chopped

2 tablespoons fish sauce

2 tablespoons lime juice

1 tablespoon sugar

2 ounces cucumber, thinly sliced

2 medium tomatoes, cut into wedges

1 medium onion, thinly sliced and
separated into rings

1 small lettuce, separated into leaves

First, boil the chicken in just enough water to cover for 10 minutes, until well cooked through. Remove from the pan and leave to cool, while continuing to boil the liquid to reduce it down to make a little concentrated stock, about 2 tablespoons only.

Meanwhile, in a bowl, prepare a dressing by mixing the garlic, shallots, chilies, fish sauce, lime juice, and sugar, adding the 2 tablespoons of reduced stock.

Place the cucumbers, tomatoes, onion, and lettuce in a large bowl. Skin the chicken and shred into the bowl. Pour the dressing over and mix thoroughly, then serve.

Serves 2 to 3.

Source: Vatch's Southeast Asian Cookbook *by Vatcharin Bhumichitr*

Glossary

ancestors people from whom a person is descended (great-grandparents, great-great-grandparents, etc.)

asylee a person who asks for asylum upon entry into the United States. Asylees may have entered the United States legally or illegally, but they have to meet the same requirements as refugees before they are granted asylum.

asylum protection or safety from persecution or the threat of persecution

capitalism an economic system in which businesses are owned by individuals and corporations rather than the government. A person who supports this type of system, especially through investments, is called a *capitalist*.

cease-fire an agreement to stop a war or violent conflict; a truce

civilization a highly developed society that demonstrates progress in the arts and sciences, keeps some form of written records, and creates political and social organizations

civil rights the rights a person has as a citizen, including protection under the law, freedom from discrimination, and freedom of speech and religion

colony an area or country under the control of another country

Communism a system of government in which the state plans and controls the economy and a single, often authoritarian party holds power, claiming to make progress toward a higher social order in which all goods are equally shared by the people

Communist a person who supports Communism

conqueror a person who gains control of a country by force

constitution a paper that states what a country's laws are and how the people will be governed

coup shortened version of *coup d'état*, the overthrow of a government, usually by a small group

culture the customs, beliefs, arts, and languages that make up a way of life for a group of people

democracy a government whose policies and leaders are directed by the people of the country

descendant a person whose descent can be traced to a particular country or ethnic group

dictator a leader who rules a country through force, often imprisoning or killing those who speak out against the government

discrimination the practice of treating people differently because of their race or other characteristics

drought long period with little or no rain

dynasty a family of powerful leaders that is maintained over generations

economy how a country makes and spends money. In a strong economy, many people have jobs and can buy what they need. In a weak economy, many people are out of work and worry about whether they will be able to pay their bills.

emigrate to leave one country to live in another

empire a group of countries, lands, or peoples under one government or ruler

ethnic group a group of people who share the same language and customs

exile having to live in another country because of political or religious reasons; a person who is forced to leave his or her country

fundamentalist describing a strict religious movement based on a literal reading of holy texts

guerrillas armed fighters, usually those who are trying to overthrow their government

hostage a person who is captured by an enemy in order to influence the opposing side's actions

immigrant a person who moves from one country to live in another

immigrate to come to a country with plans to live there

indentured laborers workers who agree to move to a new country and work for little or no pay for a certain number of years in exchange for travel expenses to the new country

migration moving from one country to live in another

nativist person or group who opposes the presence of immigrants or foreigners in the United States

network a group of people from similar backgrounds who help each other

parliament a legislative body made up of representatives

peninsula a landmass surrounded on three sides by water

plantation a large farm where crops are often grown by workers who live on the estate

protectorate a relationship in which a strong country agrees to protect a smaller country or region in return for some degree of control over the smaller country's affairs

quota system a system of determining how many immigrants can enter a country each year; each foreign country or region is assigned a quota, or maximum number of immigrants

racism prejudice based on race

rebellion armed resistance against authority, usually unsuccessful

refugee a person who seeks safety in another country due to fears of imprisonment, torture, or death because of race, religion, nationality, or political beliefs. In the United States, refugee status is granted to those who apply for resettlement in the United States while they are still in another country.

regime a particular style of government; often used to describe a government that controls its people through force or oppression

sanctions punishments, usually economic, that one country or group of countries imposes on another, such as not letting that country buy or sell certain types of goods

socialism a form of government in which the state owns all the property and businesses and people are paid according to the type of work they do

terrorists individuals or groups who use violence to intimidate or influence others, especially for political reasons

Third World countries in Latin America, Africa, and Asia that are trying to develop economic strength. First used during the Cold War, this term described developing countries that were not aligned with either the United States or the Soviet Union.

Bibliography

Ali-Dinar, Ali B., ed. "Kenya-Food." *African Studies Center—University of Pennsylvania* http://www.sas.upenn.edu/African_Studies/NEH/k-food.html

Alleyne, Mervyn C. *Roots of Jamaican Culture*. London: Pluto Press, 1990.

Ashabranner, Brent. *The New African Americans*. North Haven, CT: Linnet Books, 1999.

Batmanglij, Najmieh K. *Taste of Persia: An Introduction to Persian Cooking*. Hong Kong: Mage Publishers, 1999.

Bayer, Marcel. *Jamaica: A Guide to People, Politics, and Culture*. Translated by John Smith. New York: Monthly Review Press, 1993.

BBC News. "UK to Right 'Immigration Wrong.'" 5/7/02 http://news.bbc.co.uk/2/hi/uk_news/politics/2088560.stm

Bhumichitr, Vatcharin. *Vatch's Southeast Asian Cookbook*. New York: St. Martin's Press, 1997.

Bratman, Fred. *War in the Persian Gulf*. Brookfield, CT: Millbrook Press, 1991.

Brownlie, Alison. *Jamaica, City and Village Life*. Austin, TX: Raintree Steck-Vaughn, 1998.

Buddhist Society for Compassionate Wisdom. "Buddha's Birthday." http://www.enteract.com/~buddha/Buddha's%20Birthday.htm

Burch, Joann J. *Kenya: Africa's Tamed Wilderness*. New York: Macmillan Children's Group, 1992.

Coultrip-Davis, Deborah, and Young Sook Ramsay. *Flavors of Korea: Delicious Vegetarian Cuisine*. Summertown, TN: Book Publishing, 1998.

Cumming, David. *India*. Austin, TX: Raintree Steck-Vaughn, 1998.

Cusick, Heidi Haughy. *Soul and Spice: African Cooking in the Americas*. San Francisco: Chronicle Books, 1995.

Danquah, Meri Nana-Ama, ed. *Becoming American: Personal Essays by First Generation Immigrant Women*. New York: Hyperion, 2000.

Dunne, Máiréad, Wambui Kairi, and Eric Nyanjom. *Kenya*. Austin, TX: Raintree Steck-Vaughn, 1998.

Fadiman, Anne. *The Spirit Catches You and You Fall Down*. New York: Farrar, Straus & Giroux, 1997.

Guensburg, Carol. "Beauty, Tragedy Captured in Hmong Needlework." *(Milwaukee, Wisconsin) Journal Sentinel*, 6/16/96http://www.hmongnet.org/culture/pandau.html

Hafner, Dorinda. *Dorinda's Taste of the Caribbean*. Berkeley, CA: Ten Speed Press, 1996.

Hassig, Susan M. *Iraq*. New York: Marshall Cavendish, 1995.

Havely, Joe. "Korea's DMZ: 'Scariest Place on Earth.'" *CNN.com*, 2/20/02 http://asia.cnn.com/2002/WORLD/asiapcf/east/02/19/koreas.dmz/

Henke, Holger. *The West Indian Americans*. Westport, CT: Greenwood Press, 2001.

Hurth, Won Moo. *The Korean Americans*. Westport, CT: Greenwood Press, 1998.

Kagda, Falaq. *India*. Milwaukee: Gareth Stevens, 1997.

Kaimal, Maya. *Savoring the Spice Coast of India: Fresh Flavors from Kerala*. New York: HarperCollins, 2000.

KenyaWeb.com. "Overview of the Kenyan Economy." http://www.kenyaweb.com/economy/index.html

Kim, Hyung-chan, ed. *Distinguished Asian Americans: A Biographical Dictionary*. Westport, CT: Greenwood Press, 1999.

King, David. *Kenya: Let's All Pull Together!* New York: Benchmark Books, 1998.

King, John. *A Family from Iraq*. Austin, TX: Raintree Steck-Vaughn, 1998.

Korean American Cultural Troupe. "HanNuRi." http://www.krcla.org/english/activities/culture.htm

Lacey, Marc. "Kenya's New Government Begins Revamping Policies." *New York Times*, 01/06/03. http://www.nytimes.com/2003/01/06/international/06CND_KENY.html

Lal, Vinay. *Manas*. http://www.sscnet.ucla.edu/southasia/Culture/Archit/TajM.html

Lao Parents and Teachers Association of Minnesota. "Lao New Year" 2002. http://www.laopta.org/HOME%20PAGE/HomePage.htm

Lee, Lauren. *Korean Americans*. New York: Marshall Cavendish, 1995.

Lee, Nachee S. "Etiquette for Interacting with the Hmong." *Hmong Cultural Center,* 2000 http://www.hmongcenter.org/etforinwitle.html

——. "Information for Visitors to a Hmong Home." *Hmong Cultural Center,* 2000 http://www.hmongcenter.org/thintowatfor.html

Leepalao, Tougeu, and Nachee Lee. "Definition of Hmong New Year." *Hmong Cultural Center,* 2000 http://www.hmongcenter.org/defofhmonnew.html

Lehrer, Brian. *The Korean Americans.* New York: Chelsea House, 1996.

Leonard, Karen I. *The South Asian Americans.* Westport, CT: Greenwood Press, 1997.

Leonard, Karen, and Al Innerarity. *Growing Up in Jamaica.* Richmond, CA: BA Cross Cultural Consultants, 1990.

Lo, Ching. "Hmong American New Year 2002." *Hmong Times,* 1/15/02 http://www.hmongtimes.com/displaynews.asp?ID=281

Luckey, Lisa A. "A Caucasian Experiences the Winona Hmong New Year Celebration." *Hmong Times,* 12/1/01 http://www.hmongtimes.com/displaynews.asp?ID=211

McMahon, Suzanne (curator). "Echoes of Freedom: South Asian Pioneers in California, 1899-1965." The Library, University of California, Berkeley http://www.lib.berkeley.edu/SSEAL/echoes/echoes.html

Murray, Jocelyn. *Africa.* New York: Facts on File, 1990.

Naff, Alixa. *The Arab Americans.* Philadelphia: Chelsea House, 1999.

Park, Kyeyoung. "Korean Organizations in Queens." Asian American Center, Queens College, April 1991 http://www.qc.edu/Asian_American_Center/aac_menu/research_resources/aacre21.html

Pateman, Robert. *Kenya.* New York: Marshall Cavendish, 1993.

Rajendra, Vijeya, and Gisela Kaplan. *Iran.* New York: Marshall Cavendish, 1996.

Sachs, Susan. "From Ancient Days, a Tasty New Year; Rites of a Persian Feast Recall Homelands Left Behind." *New York Times,* 3/21/02.

Sheehan, Sean. *Jamaica.* New York: Marshall Cavendish, 1994.

Spencer, William. *Iran: Land of the Peacock Throne.* Tarrytown, NY: Benchmark Books, 1997.

Srinivasan, Radhika. *India.* New York: Marshall Cavendish, 1993.

Takaki, Ronald. *From Exiles to Immigrants.* New York: Chelsea House, 1995.

——. *From the Land of Morning Calm: The Koreans in America.* New York: Chelsea House, 1994.

U.S. Central Intelligence Agency. *The World Factbook 2002.* http://www.odci.gov/cia/publications/factbook/index.html

Virtual Hmong: Window to the Hmong People. "Hmong New Year." http://www.hmoob.com/newyear/

Viswath, R. *Teenage Refugees and Immigrants from India Speak Out.* New York: Rosen Publishing Group, 1997.

Washington State Arts Commission. "Asian American Traditional Festivals" www.arts.wa.gov/

——. "Traditions of Change: Five Korean-American Traditional Arts in Washington State" www.arts.wa.gov/

Waters, Anita M. Race, *Class and Political Symbols: Rastafari and Reggae in Jamaican Politics.* New Brunswick, NJ: Transaction Publications, Rutgers University, 1989.

Xiong, Ka Zoua. "ACC Celebrates the Hmong New Year!" *The Mural,* 10/24/02 http://www.ahs.stpaul.k12.mn.us/mural/vol1/issue2/newyear.html

Zahoor, Akram, and Z. Haq. *Taj Mahal.* http://cyberistan.org/islamic/tajmahal.html

Zickgraf, Ralph. *Laos.* Philadelphia: Chelsea House, 1999.

Index

DATE		
For Reference		
Not to be taken from this room		